THE DERMIS PROBE

THE DERMIS PROBE

IDRIES SHAH

THE OCTAGON PRESS
LONDON

Copyright © 1970, 1980 by Idries Shah

ISBN 0 863040 45 4

First impression in this Edition 1989

Printed and bound in Great Britain at
The Camelot Press Ltd., Southampton.

Contents

Preface

ͽͽͽͽͽͽͽͽͽͽͽͽͽͽͽͽͽͽͽͽͽͽͽͽͽ

GOLDFISH

A MAN once wanted to observe goldfish. His aim was to see whether some of their peculiarities could help scientists to understand certain human nervous conditions.

He found a patron to support the work and travelled to a far country to carry out his research.

Soon after he started his goldfish-watching, however, the authorities discovered that he lacked the necessary licences and certificates. By watching goldfish he had broken the law.

Although a university graduate and an expert on the psychology of fish, this man was unaware of the local regulations and the mentality of those who made and interpreted them.

In this book you can find illustrated some of the peculiarities of thought in the country which is today's world, seen by its inhabitants and by those who call themselves visitors.

If you think, incidentally, that a scientist is allowed to watch goldfish without permission, read the Report of the Home Office under the Cruelty to Animals Act, published in 1968, where the offence is officially recorded.

Institute for Cultural Research,   IDRIES SHAH
P.O. Box 13, Tunbridge Wells, Kent.

THE DERMIS PROBE

OVER eight hundred years ago, the philosopher
Hakim Majdud Sanai of Ghazna (Afghanistan), in his
Walled Garden of Truth, published this tale in a form
corresponding to the needs of his time. His pupil
and fellow-countryman, Jalaludin Rumi, immor-
talized his version in the incomparable *Mathnavi*,
towards the end of the thirteenth century. In 1965
this adaptation was filmed by the celebrated pro-
ducer-director Richard Williams on the basis of a
twentieth-century version by Idries Shah.

The film won a citation as an Outstanding Film of
the Year, being chosen for exhibition at the London
and New York Film Festivals.

THE DERMIS PROBE

The prizewinning film by Richard Williams

SCRIPT BY

IDRIES SHAH

from a story by J. D. Rumi of Konia

after H. M. Sanai, of

Ghazna

The Dermis Probe

MEMBERS of the Commission of World Scientists gaze at a bewildering sight, brought to us by television, using cameras equipped with close-up lenses of inordinate power.

The picture pans across a greyish, striated surface, a vista of solid in space, broken here and there by fissures, sometimes curving, sometimes obscured by flat shadows. Nothing moves, nothing grows on the barren area. The harsh roughness of the sight hints at a silent, empty mass, an outer skin as of a larva or a pachyderm, gnarled as though with immemorial age.

As we watch, the American commentator's voice sets the scene of this documentary report:

'From the beginning of time, man has consistently and untiringly explored his environment, he has striven to extend the threshold of his knowledge, even driving probes deep into outer space ... '

The British voice of the Chairman of the Commission is now heard, as the pictures of the object alternate, the angles varying, to give as complete a view as possible of the intimidating, silent bulk:

'What we are considering here is the, er, topography of the outer husk, as it were, the skin of the, er, bulk of a mass whose characterisics are ... '

Now fades in the matter-of-fact report of the laboratory astro-physicist, giving a fragment of his results:

' ... Microscopic sections of this undoubtedly organic material betray a cellular structure strikingly akin to Dermic tissue.'

The viewers can hear sounds corresponding with the laboratory operation. The astro-physicist continues:

'Staining the section with Von Glauben's Fluid ... '

He is interrupted, for this is a democratic discussion.

The German Scientist's rejoinder is clearly heard:

'Von Glauben's Fluid? May I point out that this was found to be a totally arbitrary method in early nineteen hundred and sixty-three, when it was superseded by Kauffer and Blakmann's Traumatic Method. It is totally out of date.'

The Chairman, like all good chairmen, switches the discussion to bring in another constructive scientist:

'Er, no, yes, er, quite; however, pending further corroboration, er, to resume, we can be safe, and, indeed, germane, in asking Professor Markarjee to give us some data on the basis of his Indian experiences with this material.'

Dr Markarjee is brisk and to the point:

'I can categorically state that positively this material cannot be conclusively classified by conventional categorization. All personnel engaged in the combined Calcutta and Benares project were objective in their subjectivity because they had been subjected to an intense programme of induced Nirvana. It is also incumbent upon me to say ... '

But time is running short, and the director of the programme fades in the unemotional voice of the American Space Expert, to give another view:

'We have recently found that the radio-carbon/90 dating of this material gives us one-two-three years on the relative timescale with a calculated error of plus or minus six point-zero. Tensile strength is directly proportional to bulk and destruct temperature demonstrates little resistance. Since this material cannot be milled or rolled, the National Aeronautics and Space Administration considers it unsuitable for the fabrication of nose-cones. It is therefore declassified.'

Now for the radio-astronomer's results:

'We have definitely established that it is not a quasi-stellar source of radio propagation, but by employing our double-basin transmitter we have been able to record marked scatter, and it could conceivably be used as a selective reflector, if a

16

substance with these characteristics were needed for advanced and extremely specialized work.'

The German Scientist, asked for his opinion again, remarks:

'But Kauffer and Blakmann have consistently shown that cellular differentiation can be more accurately demonstrated by high-magnetic differential illumination and spectroscopic micro-analysis.'

The Chairman feels that the time has come to bring the programme to a graceful end:

'Ah, well, er. I think that, er, we can all safely conclude that while knowing nothing of the overall picture, all evidence *tends to suggest* that the specific material in question, while not static and—seemingly—singularly obstructive and of a rather fibrous character, will undoubtedly reveal itself in its own good time: and, indeed, take its rightful place in the scheme of things.'

The camera zoom-lenses are beginning to retreat as the American Commentator gives his final ringing phrase:

'... And will eventually fall before Man's ever-questing search.'

While the credit lists of participants are being rolled across the picture, it is possible to see that the lenses have retracted to such an extent that, for the first time, the whole of the object, not just its skin, is visible. It is a large, African, elephant.

But the Motto of the Institute of Comparative Dermatography now nearly obscures the picture, getting larger as we read:

THE PARTS ARE GREATER THAN THE
WHOLE

Salute to the Thief

JUNAID OF Baghdad was passing the scene of a public hanging, where a thief was on the scaffold.

Junaid bowed towards the criminal.

Someone asked him:

'Why did you do that?'

Junaid said:

'I was bowing before his single-mindedness. For his aim, that man has given his life.'

*　*　*

Show a man too many camels' bones, or show them to him too often, and he will not be able to recognize a camel when he comes across a live one.

(*Mirza Ahsan of Tabriz*)

HEADQUARTERS, EARTH

Do not tell your secrets to everyone in this headquarters, Earth.

We have surveyed it well. There was nobody to whom to entrust secrets.

(*Anwar-i-Suhaili*)

The Critic

A NUMBER of disciples incessantly sang the praises of a certain Sufi teacher.

One day they surrounded the dwelling of a dervish who had criticized him.

They said:

'You have attacked and calumniated our teacher. We demand that you retract what you have said.'

He answered:

'How trivial and shallow is the reasoning of the raw! Return to your master and ask him to tell you why Arif Yahya criticizes him—for you should have done that before coming here, one exciting the other like a pack of wolves, intent only on destruction.'

The disciples retreated. When they found a suitable opportunity to talk to Si Mandoub, their mentor, he said:

'Arif Yahya opposes me so that the shallow-minded shall be influenced away from me. In this manner, he and I work together, and I am left with more peace to carry on with my undertakings.'

*   *   *

The mine is always bigger than the gem.

Proverb

The Materials of the Locality

IBN ASWAD visited the Tekkia of Sheikh Halim Unwani in Syria and was much impressed by the extent and dignity of the place, the numbers of servants and the plenitude of disciples.

Sheikh Halim was, however, absent, and Aswad followed him to North Africa, where he had settled for a number of years to spread the Teaching there.

In Morocco he found Halim living in a small house, with a mere shed outside for the exercises. His pupils numbered no more than a handful, and his clothes were of the simplest kind.

Aswad was perplexed and, taking Halim's closest associate, Mustafa Mahjub, aside, he asked him:

'Why does the Sheikh not bring people and wealth from Aleppo and Damascus, and show these people of Africa that he is a man of substance? Why does he not bring droves of disciples from the East, and carpets and workmen, and make a fitting audience-hall?'

Mahjub laughed, and then he said:

'Our gold is not the same as their gold, as our tongue sounds different from their tongue. Do you not see how our Sheikh talks and dresses like a man of the locality? The crops of the locality, the houses of the locality come from the materials of the locality.'

*   *   *

Better to quarrel with a friend than to support enemies.

Proverb

The Strange Becomes Commonplace

ᏮᏲᏮᏲᏮᏲᏮᏲᏮᏲᏮᏲᏮᏲᏮᏲᏮᏲᏮᏲᏮᏲᏮᏲᏮᏲᏮᏲᏮᏲᏮᏲᏮᏲᏮᏲ

A SCHOLAR asked the great sage Afzal of Iskandariya:

'What can you tell me of Alim Azimi, your teacher, to whom you attribute qualities which have fashioned you?'

Afzal answered:

'His poetry intoxicated me, and his love of mankind suffused me, and his self-sacrificing services elated me.'

The scholar said:

'Such a man would indeed be able to fashion angels!'

Afzal continued:

'Those are the qualities which would have recommended Alim to *you*. Now for the qualities which enabled him to help men transcend the ordinary:

'Hazrat Alim Azimi made me irritated, which caused me to examine my irritation, to trace its source. Alim Azimi made me angry, so that I could feel and transform my anger. Alim Azimi allowed himself to be attacked, so that people could see the bestiality of his attackers and not join with them. He showed us the strange, so that the strange became commonplace and we could realize what it really is.'

*   *   *

Whoever has not first dug a well, should not steal a minaret.

Proverb

Invisible Service

AJNABI USED to give away books, saying:
'I have finished with this, perhaps you would like it.'
He also gave food to people, saying:
'I am not hungry—would you like to eat?'
His companion Husseini once said to him:
'You never allow people to perceive what you are doing for them. They think that they are getting something which is of no use to you. Therefore they do not prize it.'
Ajnabi said:
'I do not expect them to prize it. In fact, I do not want them to prize it. I want them to benefit, not to adulate.'
Husseini records:
'Ajnabi gave his teachings in the same way, too. Nobody ever knew what they were learning, because he made them possessors of learning in a manner which prevented them from prizing learning. They generally thought that they were taking part in some completely irrelevant activity.
'Ajnabi used to say: "That portion of learning which people prize is precisely that part which is not doing them any good: like a sweetmeat which is admired but not eaten." '

*   *   *

None meets harm who knows his capacity.
Proverb

Dismissed

ᠬᠬᠬᠬᠬᠬᠬᠬᠬᠬᠬᠬᠬᠬᠬᠬᠬᠬᠬᠬᠬᠬᠬᠬᠬᠬᠬᠬ

ANWAR OF Badakhshan was perplexed when he visited Aleppo and found as Maulana Bahaudin's representative there a man whom the Maulana had dismissed from his presence several years before.

Anwar, when he returned to Bokhara, asked the Maulana how it could be that someone who had been the target of the teacher's wrath could find eventual acceptance in such a high position.

The Maulana said:

'The wind blows floating seeds, and makes them fly to wherever they may flourish if the possibility exists. To the outward observer, the wind may appear hostile to the seeds. But what, in such an instance, is the function of the wind, if it is not to provide the impetus which the seeds need?'

*　　*　　*

If you are covetous, you are a prisoner:
If you are greedy, you will never be filled.

Proverb

Four Communities

A SUFI master on a journey saw a number of people struggling to haul a crocodile out of a river. Seeing that the animal was not dead, and could kill some of them if they got it on shore, he cut the rope which they had attached to it.

The people seized him and beat him, crying:

'Dressed like a Sufi, he is a hypocrite as well as a wrongdoer, for Sufis only do what is good.'

Some time later, he came upon a group of dervishes who thought that by action they would attain 'being'. He told them that their 'being' would come through inaction. They put him to flight.

Subsequently he settled among a school of Seekers who were contemplatives. He realized that they needed action, so he told them:

' "Being" comes through action.'

They followed his guidance until one of the dervishes happened to call upon a friend, after which he came back and told them:

'This man is a fraud and an opportunist. He used to preach "Being comes from inaction" and was thrown out for it. So he tries the opposite argument.'

So the Seekers expelled the Sufi master.

He found another group of people, and said to them:

' "Being" comes sometimes from action and sometimes from inaction."

They answered:

'If you had only told us to act when it was time to act, we would have done so. And if you had told us not to act when it was time for inaction, we would have done so. As it is, you are confusing us, dividing our concentration. Give us one dogma at a time.'

He had to part company with them.

These were the first four communities with which he worked.

It is rumoured that he is now living in a fifth.

* * *

No surgeon can treat the wounds of the tongue.

Proverb

KINDNESS

This is a time when, because of excessive wrongs,
It is impossible to be safe in life and goods.
Of whom can we think well when it is believed
That if nothing bad is done to you, this has been
a kindness?

(*Anwar-i-Suhaili*)

Accumulated Supplications

IT WAS an established custom in a certain place for people to visit a shrine, and to pray there for good fortune.

They gave a small offering to the dervish who looked after the place, towards his upkeep and for charity.

After many years of this tradition, whose very origin had by then been forgotten, a really needy man arrived.

But he asked for nothing.

At the moment of his arrival, a charitable individual came upon him. The charitable man said:

'I have made a vow to give away all my money at this place to the first person I meet.'

He bestowed every penny of his wealth upon the truly needy man.

One of the disciples of the dervish asked the inner meaning of this transaction.

The dervish, full of wisdom, told him:

'The accumulated supplications were waiting for a needy man who did not ask. As soon as he appeared, the right aspirations operated and the prayers were able to take a true effect.'

'But the people believe that the shrine itself brings them good fortune,' objected a bystander.

'It brings good fortune to those worthy of it. The unworthy attribute their luck to having been at the shrine. But attribution is often different from origin.'

Opinion and Fact

A GREAT teacher who knew the way to wisdom was visited by a group of Seekers.

They found him in his courtyard, surrounded by disciples, in the midst of revels.

Some of the observers said:

'How obnoxious— this is no way to behave, whatever the pretext.'

Others said:

'This seems to us excellent— we like this kind of teaching, and wish to take part in it.'

Yet others said:

'We are partly perplexed and wish to know more about this puzzle.'

The rest said to one another:

'There may be some wisdom in this, but whether we should ask about it or not we do not know.'

The teacher sent them all away.

And these people all spread, in conversation and in writing, their opinions of the occasion. Even those who did not allude to their experience directly were affected by it, and their speech and even actions reflected their feelings about it.

Some time later certain members of this party again passed that way. They called upon the teacher.

They stood at his door, observing that within the courtyard he and his students now sat, decorously, deep in contemplation.

'This is better,' said some of the visitors, 'for he has learned from our protests.'

'This is excellent,' said others, 'the last time he was undoubtedly only testing us.'

27

'This is too sombre,' said others, 'surely we can find long faces anywhere.'

And there were other opinions, spoken and otherwise.

The great sage, when the time of reflection was over, sent all these visitors away.

Much later, a small number returned and sought his interpretation of what they had experienced.

They presented themselves at the gate and looked into the courtyard. The teacher sat there, alone, neither revelling nor in meditation. His former disciples were nowhere to be seen.

'You may now hear the whole story,' he said, 'for I have been able to dismiss my disciples; the task is done.

'When you first came here, that class of mine had been too serious—I was in the process of applying the corrective. The second time you came, they had been too gay—I was applying the corrective.

'When a man is working he does not always explain himself to casual visitors, however interested the visitors may think themselves to be. When an action is in progress, what counts is the correct operation of that action. Under these circumstances, external evaluation becomes a secondary concern. What people may imagine about something is more descriptive of themselves than of the situation.'

*   *   *

RUST

Rust through washing never became white.

(*Anwar-i-Suhaili*)

Full Circle

HOW DID Odi Odam come to sit at the feet of the Wise One, Dervish Rahim?

He roused himself one day and thought, as the sun shone in his eyes, 'It is more than time that I achieved something.'

So he looked around for ideas, and his eyes lighted upon a book in the corner of the room. It had been lying there for years, since his late father's time, but he had not paid much attention to it before.

'This should do for a start,' he told himself, 'for has it not been laid down by the scholars that "To do something is better than to do nothing at all"?'

He picked up the book and carried it to the near-by town. In the market-place a man came up to him and said, 'What special virtue has that book, and what price do you place upon it?'

'Why,' said Odi Odam, 'it was my father's, and that surely means that it is of the greatest worth. Do you not respect the judgment of your own father?'

'Of course,' said the other man. And he gave Odi all that he had for the book.

Odi next saw a man sitting beside a pile of feathers in the street. He had just plucked a fowl and sold it, and the feathers were left over. 'What special virtue have your feathers, and what price do you place upon them?' asked Odi.

The man was rather less than honest, and he said, 'You can have them for all the money you have. As to their virtue, I may not tell you.' There was a local law against making false claims about merchandise.

Odi gave the man everything he had, and took the feathers, thinking, 'If they have a secret value, there will be a way to discover it. The most important thing is possession, not information.'

He was remembering the advice of the tradition which says:

'Information may not lead to possession, but possession may lead to information.'

But then he met a fool with an engaging manner, who said to him:

'I wish I had feathers like them, then I might be able to become a bird. But I am poor.'

'Do you know about the secret virtue of feathers?' asked Odi.

'No,' said the fool, and he did not.

'In that case', said Odi, 'you will not have the advantage of me if I part with them. What can you trade, friend?'

'What about this book, which a man just threw at me because I annoyed him?' said the fool.

Odi saw that it was his father's book.

He took it in exchange for the feathers, but he could not read, so he took it to the Dervish Rahim.

Dervish Rahim said:

'This book is called "Never wander about exchanging one thing for another. If you do, you will be one in a million if you get a second chance to make a real start." '

*   *   *

Whoever is to be wise despises himself. Only the ignorant trust their own judgment.

Proverb

The Insane

AJNABI SAID:

'The people of this world are insane.'

He promised his disciples to give them evidence of this.

That same night he invited a rich man to break the fast with him. The man came and they ate dry bread and a date apiece, which was all that Ajnabi had in the house.

When he returned home, the rich man sent the Sufi a purse containing ten thousand dinars. Ajnabi sent it back with a note saying, 'Bread can be eaten, gold is not useful for anything—people only imagine that it is.'

Now he called a needy man and sent him to the rich man's house to ask for ten thousand dinars. When the man came back, Ajnabi said, 'What did he say?'

The needy man said:

'He told me that he would not give me anything.'

Then Ajnabi told his disciples:

'The people of this world are assuredly insane. They think that gold is equal to bread, and even exchange one for the other. Then, when they see an honest and necessitous man, they imagine that it is in their own interests not to help him. If these people are sane, as they believe themselves to be, let us all hasten into what they would call insanity.'

*   *   *

Whoever has taught me one letter has made me his slave.

Proverb

A Group of Sufis

A GROUP of Sufis, sent by their preceptor to live and work in a certain district, settled themselves in a house.

In order to avoid undesirable attention, only the man in charge—the Chief Deputy—taught in public. The rest of the community outwardly assumed the functions of servants of the household.

When the Deputy died, the members of the community rearranged their functions, revealing themselves as advanced mystics, in accordance with their instructions from the original preceptor.

But the inhabitants of the country not only shunned them as imitators, but actually said, 'For shame! See how they have usurped and distributed the patrimony of the Great Teacher. Why, these miserable hirelings now even behave as if they were themselves Sufis!'

*   *   *

The tongue is the best masseur of furrowed brows.

(*Anwar-i-Suhaili*)

Salik on the Road to Qandahar

SALIK MET a party of men on the highway to Qandahar. Salik was dressed like a tanner, and one of the party, who was greatly respected by them, was wearing the robe of a Sufi.

Salik asked him, 'What are you?'

The man answered, 'A Sufi.'

Salik immediately drew a long knife and advanced towards the man, who showed every sign of fear. 'Why are you trembling?' asked Salik.

'I fear you may kill me,' said the other man.

'Will you give me your money if I spare your life?' asked Salik.

'Yes, indeed,' said the other.

Salik now addressed the rest of the party:

'This man is no Sufi. He is afraid of death and will give money in return for life. A Sufi is one who cannot be manipulated by fear or desire.'

*　　*　　*

Make mankind your dwelling-place.

(*Hariri*)

Absent

⦿⦿⦿⦿⦿⦿⦿⦿⦿⦿⦿⦿⦿⦿⦿⦿⦿⦿⦿⦿⦿⦿⦿⦿⦿⦿

THE SUFI master Halqavi was dared to go into the presence of a certain king and immediately say something negative, a mark of disrespect which would be likely to cost him his life.

He accepted the challenge without any hesitation.

As soon as he was shown into the throne-room, the king— a capricious character—said:

'Since you are reputed to be so clever, I order you, for my amusement, to say something which nobody who is present can ever say.'

Without the slightest pause, the Sufi said:

'I am not in your presence.'

*　　*　　*

FROM THE BEGINNING ...

From the beginning, from the age of Adam to the time of kingship:

From the powerful, pardon: from the poor, sins.

(*Anwar-i-Suhaili*)

Three Sufi Masters

A Sufi sage was sitting among his followers when a newcomer, accustomed to the ways of the Court, entered and began to praise the teacher. The disciples listened attentively, and the man continued his compliments.

In the meantime a second sage entered, listened for a time, and then began to shout insults at the first master.

The visitor withdrew in confusion, while the first master sat impassively until the second sage had left.

A third Sufi master entered the company after some time, and one of the disciples made a sign indicating that he wished to ask a question.

'The third master will answer it,' said the first sage.

'Why was our teacher reviled by the second master, since both are of equal eminence, and our teacher is not worthy of such abuse?' asked the disciple.

'A visitor from the world was here, filling the air with false compliments,' said the third master, 'and these were so beastly in their effect, if not their appearance, that it needed something equally beastly to drive them from the air.'

* * *

DEATH

If he is a good man, death will be a release;
If he is a bad one, it will release others from him.

(*Anwar-i-Suhaili*)

Secret Knowledge

THE *Khalifa* (Deputy) of a certain Sufi teacher enlisted in the mystical exercises everyone whom he could find. Many who came to hear of this objected, saying, 'Is it not repeatedly said by the Sufis that only those who can profit may have the exercises, for otherwise this is not Sufism?'

He answered:

'It is also said, "The profit and loss are assessed at the end of the day's trade, not at the beginning." ' And he continued to recruit all and sundry.

Every day he questioned the followers, asking them if they were serious and sincere. All swore that they were. But he found many disparities between their words and their actions.

So he stopped talking to them at all, saying, 'I cause you to sin if I ask you to aver something and you lie.' Many of them left him in disgust, saying, 'We are not hypocrites,' though they were.

He criticized those who remained, and many more started to drift away.

Then he pretended to be mad, and quite a number of the remaining disciples abandoned him, the more charitable saying, 'Poor fellow, he would have been perfect had he not been insane.'

Now came the day when there were only six students left.

One of them said:

'I suppose that these are the ones who have passed the test, and who will now be taught by the master himself?'

'No,' said the Deputy, 'unfortunately only some of these are real disciples. The others are those who are so obsessed by the search for secret knowledge—are in fact so greedy for themselves—that they will do anything and endure anything. Before I present the final selection to our master I shall have to expel those—or have them expel themselves.'

* * *

BRANCHES

The barren branches may appear inelegant: They are, to the cook, the means to make his fire.

(Anwar-i-Suhaili)

PROVISION AND LIFE

They have fixed our nutrition and arranged our life-span. More than this, and ahead of this, efforts will not be productive.

(Anwar-i-Suhaili)

The Mob

A CERTAIN Sufi once said to his followers:

'We shall now practise the burning of the objects connected with our studies, the denunciation of the principles which all consider to be central to our beliefs, and the carrying out of the dervish science in places other than the customary ones.'

Taking this as a test of faith, many of his followers obeyed. Some even said:

'How sublime that we should be learning to abandon externals, for this is surely a means of concentrating our attention upon essentials.'

A few years after this there was a great commotion in the city in which this community was living. Someone came to them and said:

'A decree has been passed declaring our activities illegal. Dervishes are being taken to prison, mobs and police are destroying our centres. We are unable to protect our property.'

'Have no fear', said the Sufi to his disciples, 'for our moment has now come.'

And when the mobs instigated by the tyrant of the country arrived a few minutes later, they did not pause, but swept past looking for victims. There was nothing that they could do at the Sufi's headquarters, for they could see that he and his people were busily dismantling it, and feeding bonfires with their property. By behaving as a mob the community maintained itself intact, and its members went free.

They are the only survivors of the students of Sufism from that entire country.

Invisible

A WELL-KNOWN Sufi was asked, 'What is invisibility?'

He said:

'I shall answer that when an opportunity for a demonstration of it occurs.'

Some time later that man and the one who had asked him the question were stopped by a band of soldiers.

The soldiers said:

'We have orders to take all dervishes into custody, for the king of this country says that they will not obey his commands, and say things which are not welcome to the tranquillity of thought of the populace.'

The Sufi said:

'And so you should, for you must do your duty.'

'But are you not Sufis?' asked the soldiers.

'Test us,' said the Sufi.

The officer took out a Sufi book. 'What is this?' he said.

The Sufi looked at the title-page.

'Something which I will burn in front of you, since you have not already done so,' he said.

He set light to the book, and the soldiers rode away, satisfied.

The Sufi's companion asked:

'What was the purpose of that action?'

'To make us invisible,' said the Sufi, 'for to the man of the world, "visibility" means that you are looking like something or someone he expects you to resemble. If you look different your true nature becomes invisible to him.'

Ahmed Yasavi

WHEN YASAVI started to teach, he was soon surrounded by potential disciples and people of all descriptions. They all listened to what he had to say, but they insisted more and more loudly on him enrolling them in a regular teaching curriculum.

Yasavi told them that he wanted them to build a special structure, a Tekkia, in which people could carry out exercises, similar to those which were found throughout Turkestan.

Several hundred people worked, under his directions, for six months, making this edifice.

When it was complete, Yasavi said:

'All who want to enter this building for instruction please stand to the right, over there; and those who do not want to do so, stand over there, to the left.'

When they were arranged in the two groups, Yasavi said:

'I dismiss all those who stand to the right: there is nothing I can do for you; therefore return whence you came.

'The remainder may become my students. Their first task is to demolish the Tekkia.'

The dismissed students became disaffected, and spread tales to the effect that Yasavi was insane. But it is from the selectivity of this madman of God that the Teaching of the Masters is derived.

*   *   *

The touchstone knows what is gold.

(*Gulistan*)

The Steam of the Pot of Ikhtiari

JUST BEFORE leaving for India, Sheikh Abu-Ali el-Ikhtiari visited all the Sufi Sheikhs of Baghdad. He told them:

'If people come from afar seeking the Way, tell them that you do not know me; and welcome them as travellers or shed them, for I shall have encouraged them only for a purpose.'

He went to India and lectured on the Way to Knowledge.

People asked him where he came from, and he always said: 'Baghdad, the Centre of Saintliness.'

Presently, in ones and twos, in caravans and in all manner of ways, Indians began to descend upon the city of Baghdad.

All the Sufis answered their questions by saying:

'We do not know Sheikh Ikhtiari,' or 'We have heard of him, certainly.'

Jafar Zikariah was present when Abdulqadir Mustafa remarked, after the visit of an Indian delegation:

'How delightful to help Sheikh Ikhtiari by being "ignorant" of him!'

A visitor asked:

'We all know the Presence Ikhtiari. How do we help his work by being "ignorant" of it?'

Sheikh Mustafa replied:

'These people are merely the "steam from Sheikh Ikhtiari's pot". They have left the stew, and imagine that they are being improved by going somewhere else.

'If we say that we know Ikhtiari, they will return and plague him, having verified that he is well thought of in his native town. If we "do not know him", they will either leave him in peace as "worthless" or else attach themselves to someone else and plague that man instead. In either case, Ikhtiari remains free.'

The Journey

'I was sitting in the circle of Sheikh Abbas Ansari one day when a youth came in and asked for help. "I am going on a journey", he said, "and I would be grateful if you could give me introductions to the Sufis of Persia."

'The Sheikh inquired as to the young man's route. Then he said, "I am sorry, I cannot give you any introductions." The visitor went sorrowfully away.

'As soon as he had gone, the Sheikh started dictating letters to his representatives in Persia, on the route named by the young man.

'I wanted to ask him the reason for this extraordinary behaviour, but the etiquette of the sessions prevented it.

'Several evenings later, when we were gathered together after a contemplation session, Sheikh Abbas said to us all:

' "If I had told that young man to visit certain of our friends, and that he would be welcomed, he would have been unable to learn, because I would have removed from his mind the determination to struggle without which he could not have benefited from the meetings. I would also have given him an increased expectation— which would have been a barrier to his understanding."

'I said:

' "But will he not think that he is unworthy and perhaps not attempt to make the journey?"

' "If he does that, it would be a sign that he is in any case lacking in the necessary resolution, and he would not have succeeded in anything."

'I asked:

42

' "But will he perhaps think of you as not interested in his welfare, since you refused to help?"

'The sheikh answered:

' "If he can turn against me so easily, then he cannot in any case learn. He would be like a dog which is refused a bone, and which would snap at whoever refused him, without thinking why."

'I said:

' "Is it undesirable for someone to feel gratitude towards another for his help?"

' "Gratitude towards another has a limit. To rely too much on the help of another leads to despising oneself and ends in opposition towards that other person. That is one reason why some people oppose those whom they have once admired. They owe them too much." '

* * *

SEPARATIONS AND MEETINGS

Separations are better than unhappy meetings.

(Anwar-i-Suhaili)

Do not carry your year's burden on one day.

Proverb

Patience is a garment which has never worn out.

(Akhlaq-i-Mohsini)

I Don't Know

NAZINDA, a dervish wanderer from Bokhara, often used to say 'I don't know' when people asked him questions.

In Allahabad, a discussion arose between those who said that a teacher should not admit ignorance of anything, and those who said that that was avowedly ignorant and was not worth discussing, and those who held various other points of view about the matter.

The arguments were submitted to the Hindu Pandit Ram Lal, who said:

'When he says "I do not know", he may mean that nobody knows. He may mean, again, that *you* do not know—he is at that moment showing your own self to you. He may mean that he does not *need* to know, because the question or the answer is fallacious.'

Someone asked, 'Why does he not put it more specifically?'

The Pandit said, 'If he did that he would cease to provoke thought and discussion.'

*   *   *

There is a marrow in every bone, there is a man in every shirt.

(*Saadi*)

How Kashmir got its Name

∞∞∞∞∞∞∞∞∞∞∞∞∞∞∞∞∞∞∞∞∞∞∞∞∞∞

THE LEGEND runs that the place now called Kashmir was previously known as Beluristan, the Land of Crystal. A certain Pandit, whose name is now forgotten, was the spiritual teacher of this country, and people from everywhere used to go to follow his exercises and learn his wisdom.

Then, one day, a descendant of the Prophet, a man of great knowledge, called a Mir in those parts, arrived to see the Pandit. He had one or two conversations with him, and then withdrew to a certain valley not far off. The Pandit said, 'He will try to displace me, but there is little chance of this, for our shrine has been known to the East and West for many centuries.' And he waited to see what the Mir would do.

The Mir, far from setting up a shrine, started a fair, with swings and a marriage-market, fortune-tellers and entertainers of all kinds. Drawn by this attraction, the followers of the Pandit made the Mir's revels the place of their nightly meetings, until the *darshan* (assembly) of the Pandit was generally unattended, and the flowers before his altar withered and were not replaced.

Finally the Pandit, attended by his few remaining followers, went up the hill to the Mir's abode, and challenged him, saying:

'You have taken away my people by deceit; and, far from even inculcating in them good conduct and correct thought of any variety, you have imported into our country a form of licence and reckless abandonment of spiritual values which makes us stand aghast.'

The Mir answered:

'Neither could you provide entertainment for your people,

45

nor could you bind them to your person. To call them "my people" in itself speaks ill of you.

'If you had imprisoned their minds, they would have regarded me and my activities as evil: but you have not done this — this much you have achieved. If you had, however, provided "your people" with anything other than diversions which you call exercises, they would not so easily have accepted my entertainment. After all, yours is free and they pay for mine.'

'Nay,' said the Pandit, 'it is rather that they are weak, and your activities have played upon their weakness.'

'If they are weak,' responded the Mir, 'and you cannot strengthen them, anyone or anything will "play upon this weakness". Why are you not a strength for the weak, rather than a toy for the credulous?'

It was at this moment that the Pandit, whose calm had been completely shattered by this unaccustomed experience, cried out the curse 'Kash-Mir!', the local pronunciation for the words Kaj-Mir, Crooked-Mir, or Devious Leader.

'If this is devious,' said the Mir, 'then I would like this land to be known, as a matter of honour, henceforward not as Beluristan, but as Kashmir, the Land of the Indirect.'

*   *   *

Learn about hornets from those who have been stung by them.

Proverb

The Way which seems To Lead To Worthlessness...

IT IS related of the Hazrat (Bahaudin Naqshband):

That although he was for many years regarded as the very incarnation of gravity and politeness in public, and the restorer of the original school of Sufism, he often behaved like a clown when with close and influential associates.

For decades he swore them to secrecy about this, and obtained from each one a signed statement that he was given to eccentric behaviour.

Time and again they said to him, 'Hazrat, we do not understand your peculiarity. But we will tell nobody about it. Why, therefore, do you accumulate evidence about it, signed documents which might at any time be produced in public to your disadvantage?'

He never answered these queries until, towards the end of his life, burdened by the weight of grave and dignified followers who insisted upon their version of his weightiness, he started to act in an unconventional manner.

Some of his more determined and most superficial followers were told to leave him. They said, 'Alas, he is taking leave of his senses! To think that he was for so long such a paragon of conduct, and an example to the whole world ... '

Then Bahaudin produced the documents which showed that he had always been of the same nature, and that it was the followers who had tried to make him into their own image of a man of the teaching.

He says in his *Risalat* (Letters), 'It is of the greatest importance that the Sufi should be able to be a fool and still be a Sufi. He must be able to appear an idiot, because when pedants monopolize the role of man of learning, there must be people among whom *real* learning subsists. Mark one danger: opposition to Sufis is not dangerous to them, because there will always be some people who will think that the opposition is due to jealousy and will therefore continue to try to follow the Way. But as soon as the scholars succeed in making people think that Sufis are devoid of serious consideration, not worth anything, people will not listen to Sufis, because if man has a weakness it is not to want to seem as if he is interested in anything worthless. Keep open the road which seems to lead to things of no consequence, viewed from the pedant's and the fanatic's eyes.'

*   *   *

THE HEAVENS
To the mallet of the Highest Mind
The heavens are the smallest possible ball.

(*Akhlaq-i-Mohsini*)

THE BIRD AND THE WATER
A bird which has not heard of fresh water
Dips his beak in salt-water year after year.

(*Anwar-i-Suhaili*)

Anwar

I WAS present with Anwar Afifi, writes Iftikhari, when a visitor was announced.

This man asked if he could be given success in a commercial venture.

Afifi said to me, 'Tell him of your experience.'

I said, 'When I first entered this place, I asked Hazrat Anwar Afifi for my children to be obedient to me and to carry out my wishes. When I arrived home, all my children were behaving in an exemplary manner. I caused them to be educated in the professions which I had chosen for them, and they invariably acquiesced.

'But, within six years of taking up those vocations, each one of them had become poor or disgraced or was dead.

'After trying to settle my own affairs for some years, I returned here. Now I am enrolled in the caravan of Anwar Afifi. My question to him nowadays is always: ''Give me what I need, and allow me to do what I can do.'' '

The visitor said:

'What ridiculous talk is this? I came for help and I get an invitation to join beggars.'

Anwar said:

'We cannot, alas, give you that invitation, however hospitable we may wish to be. You came for help, but all we can give you is information. The kind of help you want is beyond our meagre store. The beggar can only give what he is allowed by others.'

Qualities

KHIDR ONCE met a pious man and said to him:

'What can I do for you?'

The man said:

'Do nothing for me — but, on your travels, help my disciples.'

Khidr asked him:

'How shall I know them?'

'By their names,' said the pious man, 'which I shall give you.'

'We of the invisible world', said Khidr, 'do not recognize people by their names, but by their qualities.'

'There is no difficulty about that', said the pious man, 'for I can list the qualities of my three disciples. The first is charitable, the second is abstemious, and the third is master of himself.'

Khidr promised, saying, 'It is in any case my duty, as a member of the invisible government, to aid such as those.'

Soon afterwards, Khidr came across a man who was almost penniless, and saw him give his last coin to a deserving woman. But Khidr passed by without helping him. Then he paused to watch a man who was lecturing people on abstention, and praying for divine aid in his work. Khidr did nothing for him. Finally, Khidr saw a man jumping for joy at being alive, even though he had a terrible disability. Khidr did not approach him.

When Khidr returned from his journey around the earth, he again met the first pious man, who said:

'Did you encounter my disciples and help them?'

Khidr answered:

'I had to help all the deserving people whom I met. But I did not see three worthy ones such as you mentioned to me.'

'Would you describe any whom you could not help?' asked the pious man.

Khidr told him about the three.

'But those are the men of whom I spoke!' said the pious man.

'If this is what you have taught them to do,' said Khidr, 'you may be pious, but you are sadly astray.

'The first man was giving away money and enjoying the act, which therefore repaid him immediately in kind—he is not charitable. The second man was only abstemious in some things: he was greedy for conversion and divine favour, and did not abstain from that greed. The third man is master of certain things, but certainly not of himself.'

*   *   *

THE PEOPLE

It is the people who are God's family.

(*Mohammed the Prophet*)

Anwar Abbasi

ᏯᏚᏯᏚᏯᏚᏯᏚᏯᏚᏯᏚᏯᏚᏯᏚᏯᏚᏯᏚᏯᏚᏯᏚᏯᏚᏯᏚᏯᏚᏯᏚᏯᏚᏯᏚᏯᏚ

ANWAR ABBASI was famous for his poetry and playing of the sitar. People went almost every evening to his home to listen to him. After the performances, some stayed behind to hear him on the subject of the Eastern philosophy (*hikmat i mashriqiyya*).

Those who went to visit him regarded Abbasi as the very exemplar of cultivation, and one whose unfailing courtesy was a model to be studied.

When, however, he was invited out to other people's houses, he employed quite a different kind of behaviour. At house after house he would annoy distinguished guests. He appeared late, interrupted learned discourses, and challenged the opinions of at least one person at every gathering.

One day he announced that his teaching mission was complete, and that he would thenceforward have no contact with people who wanted to learn. He left the country, and was never seen there again.

Those who were perplexed at his behaviour went to Firoz Andaki, long known as his chief opponent, and asked for enlightenment.

Firoz said, 'You want me to criticize Abbasi: but I have to tell you that it is only recently that I have learned how great a man he was. I regard him as my teacher, and I will tell you something of the grandeur of his teaching by example and demonstration, vast distances beyond our general level of comprehension.

'Abbasi cared so little for his reputation that he threw it away as fuel for the flame of his teaching. When he started arguments, nine out of ten people said, "How uncouth!" but

the tenth said, "He is showing us all the absurdity of argument."

'In preference to establishing fame and respect among men,
he established real teaching for those who could accept it.'

*   *   *

Poor greedy one, wherever he runs
He's after food, and death is after him.

(*Saadi*)

You may be able to get the bone down your throat
But if it reaches your stomach it will tear your navel.

(*Gulistan*)

Learning without action is like wax without honey.

(*Anwar-i-Suhaili*)

Protection

It is related that someone said to Sahl:

'Many entirely worthy people oppose what you say and do. It has been said that this is because you do not compromise with them, and the progress of understanding of the Sufi Path is hindered thereby. Would it be appropriate to ask for clarification of this?'

Sahl said:

'The only way in which the People of the Path can protect the Way and the disciples from narrow thinkers and destructive elements is to become unacceptable to such people. A wild animal will leave you alone if it dislikes you, so you must cause aversion if you cannot otherwise protect yourself from it. So when people say, "You have tried to explain yourself to me and have failed," this may mean, "Unknown to me, you have made me avoid you, for the purpose of maintaining your own tranquillity." '

*　　*　　*

Even if false gold makes a man happy:
At the mint it will be identified.

(*Rumi*)

The Aristocrat

IMAM YUSUF of Samarkand relates:

I studied the records of the miracles and the reputes of the Hashemite Clan, and decided that it could not be accidental or entirely imagined that they contained such a frequent number of spiritually elevated men.

Eventually I decided to approach Sayed Nuri Shah-i-Husseini, who lived in a glorious palace, surrounded by every luxury, and made my way to him.

He admitted me to his company, but whenever I turned the conversation to his heritage as a guardian of the knowledge of the inner government, he changed the subject.

At length I said to him:

'Lord of Princes! Your repute and attraction is based upon the well-known fact of your descent from the Elect Family. Why, then, will you never discuss this theme?'

He said:

'You have tracked me down by means of my tracks. Are we still to discuss these "marks on the snow or sand", or are you here to learn?'

I was amazed by this thought, and immediately realized that he was right, and what others thought about this science was shallow. So I became bold enough to ask the other question which puzzled me:

'How can a master of spirituality live in such luxury, when it is not traditional?'

He said:

'Have you ever seen me take any advantage of the surroundings?'

I said, 'No, I have not.'

He said, 'In that case I can reveal to you, to be concealed

until my death, that there are two forms of concealment: hiding oneself and living in an atmosphere which protects you by incongruity.'

*   *   *

A loan is the scissors of friendship.
A man's own tongue may cut his throat.
The cage has no value without the bird.

(Saadi)

UNLUCKY

Call yourself unlucky only if you take up coffin-making and people stop dying.

Proverb

Grief and Joy

THEY SAID to a Dervish master:

'You make yourself appear ridiculous to outward observers. This causes grief to your friends and joy to your opponents, who can easily represent you as a nonentity.'

He answered:

'O friends born to attain felicity! You have seen half, and think that you have seen all; and this is the last time that I shall explain. I look foolish to the people whom I wish to discourage. If my friends were real friends they would seek this explanation, and not feel grief. By causing joy to my opponents, I am giving them a chance to realize that their joy is misplaced, and based on superficial assessment.'

*   *   *

The spirit is the mirror; the body is the rust.
(*Divan-i-Shamsi Tabriz*)

No effort makes a black crow into a white hawk.
(*Anwar-i-Suhaili*)

The Magician

THERE WAS once a man who travelled all over the world and studied in every place of real learning.

Because of his retiring ways, opinions were for long divided as to whether he was a devout and worthy man or whether perhaps he was some kind of magician, alchemist or even astrologer; a follower of reprehensible arts.

Consequently, his house was besieged by two kinds of people: those who sought his blessing if he were to be revealed as a man of learning, and those who wanted to enlist his aid in some mundane enterprise, should they discover that he was possessed of secret arts.

This man, known by the name of Abdulwahid, son of Aswad, eventually acquired the repute of a sorcerer and necromancer. The consequence was that people who imagined that they were sincere and praiseworthy shunned him. Those who sought the help of a sorcerer continued to seek him out.

When, however, the potential magicians and buyers of talismans and charms entered his presence, he soon sent them away. He did this by convincing them that he only pretended to be a magician. In this way he was able to shed them more rapidly and completely than would otherwise have been possible.

Hence to his ordinary repute of magical activity was added the charge, spread by the disappointed, of charlatanism, even in that doubtful vocation.

This man was in fact a Sufi. He discouraged the passionate believers in their own sincerity because such people are almost always only superficially sincere. Their reality is self-deception, and they are more difficult to help than those who have no such prejudice in their own favour. Their belief was stronger than their sincerity.

Ibn Aswad's beneficent influence and the results of his work continue. But, because of his methods of self-concealment and self-defence, few Sufis may now mention the debt which everyone in the world owes to Abdulwahid, son of Aswad.

*   *   *

Much smoke has been seen, and caused great fear of fire— even when no fire ensued.

Proverb

Opportunity's precious, and time is a sword.

(Saadi)

To bind one free man with love is better than to release a thousand slaves.

(Omar Khayyam)

Grammar

A SCHOLAR who was also a noted grammarian went to see a Sufi teacher.

He was surprised to find that the Sufi did not lecture, cajole or advance carefully constructed proofs for what he was doing.

When he had the opportunity, he asked the Sufi:

'Why do you not teach in a coherent manner? You must know the simple beginnings of your lore as well as the more abstruse aspects. We scholars at least take note of the ignorance of beginners, and lead them by degrees from simple things into advanced knowledge.'

The Sufi said:

'I can illustrate this to you only if you will undertake a short course of instruction, and ask no questions.'

The Sufi was a man of such repute that it was believed that he could work miracles. Because the scholar was hungry for knowledge, he agreed.

The Sufi said:

'You are a grammarian. Very well: every day you shall collect the local cats and dogs and lecture them on the very earliest and most simple aspects of grammar.'

Thinking that this was a test, or that it would lead to a miracle, the scholar obeyed.

After several months the Sufi called the scholar to him and said:

'Have the cats and dogs learned any grammar?'

'No,' said the grammarian, 'none at all.'

'Why do you suppose that this is the case?'

'Because they cannot speak or understand speech. They have to learn that first, if it is possible.'

'That is the answer to your original question,' said the Sufi master.

* * *

An old fool is worse than a young one:
For the young may always grow wise.

(Zohair)

COINCIDENCE

The Sage said:

'Fate continues. But on no account abandon your own intentions.

'For if your plans accord with the Supreme Will you will attain a plenitude of fulfilment for your heart.'

(*Anwar-i-Suhaili*)

Dissatisfied

A SUFI once met a dissatisfied monk leaving the place of audience of Maulana Bahaudin Naqshband.

The monk said:

'Shun that man, for he will only occupy himself with trivia. I have travelled from China to drink his wisdom, and he offers me a children's tale!'

When the Sufi entered the presence of the teacher, the Maulana said, as if reading his mind:

'There are a thousand books of classics, all written to illustrate a dozen truths. There are a dozen tales which contain within them all those truths. If it were not for the demand of many for the appearance of quantity rather than relevance, the first letter of the first word of a single children's story could suffice to instruct man.

'It is because the learner is of such poor quality that the teacher has to repeat, enlarge and make bulky things which the student would not otherwise be able to see at all.'

* * *

When sense has left a head, it should be called a tail.

(*Rumi*)

Conviction

TALAL NAZAF was received with great honour at the Court of Cordoba. His reputation had been known there for many years: courtiers and Emirs vied with one another to speak well of him.

A certain scholar, however, asked him this question:

'I have read your books and wonder why so much in them is directed towards the stupid, and so little towards the wise.'

Talal said:

'Most of it is directed towards such as you.'

That evening he was taking a meal at the house of the Grand Qadi (judge), who remarked, with delicacy:

'A certain robustness of speech here in Cordoba might cause those who are well-disposed, and yet sensitive, to change their attitude towards a newcomer.'

The Sufi said:

'Those who have observed that such sensitivity, acted upon by forthrightness, produces hostility, have learned that such a change is merely a change of opinion.

'I am here to demonstrate that a change of opinion is in itself not a change of understanding. Opinion is built upon sand. Knowledge is built upon rock. If a man is only convinced that I am good, he may be as stupid as one who is only convinced that I am bad.

'Conviction, far from being based upon reason, is the enemy of reason; because rationality does not change, while convictions do, all the time.'

The Light-Taker

A CERTAIN dervish was called Nourgir— 'light-taker'— because he had a clay pot which took in light from the day, even from a candle, and gave it out when he wanted it to.

He was asked by a scholar:

'We do not deny the remarkable characteristics of your light-trapping pot. But we do question your rumoured capacity to see into the hearts of men.

'If you can indeed perceive people's characters and potentialities, how is it that someone has just sold you a melon which proved to be tasteless?'

Nourgir said:

'Would you care to come with me and undertake an experiment?'

This scholar refused, and spread the word that Nourgir was a charlatan. But, after many months of this defamation, they both found themselves at the court of the king of the time, and the king showed interest in the dispute.

The king said:

'It has been conveyed to my ears that this scholar has challenged this dervish, but that he will not allow the dervish to demonstrate his capacities. Such an attitude is a menace to good order and a threat to the general tranquillity of men. The scholar will stand condemned as a jackal, so pronounced by me, unless he agrees to stop talking about facts, and allows himself to be exposed to realities. I cannot think that he will reveal himself to be the word-drudge that people must conclude him to be if he were to rely upon uninformed opinion for his proofs, to resort to spleen and personal calumny, or to do any of the other things which mark the pretended, as distinct from the real, scholar.'

The dervish and scholar said, 'We hear and obey.'

The dervish took the scholar to the top of a mountain and made him stay with him for three days, listening to dervish lore. Then he brought him down to a defile in the mountains where a crowd of witnesses were waiting, headed by the king.

People were toiling up the track, on horses and mules, with donkeys and on foot, and as they approached, the dervish said:

'Look, King and Scholar. I shall place my hand on the shoulder of this scholar, lending him some of my perceptiveness. As each person nears yonder bend he will become aware of their inner thoughts. His awareness will answer his question as to why a dervish does not use his powers all the time.'

Sure enough, as person after person passed the appointed spot, the scholar's face became more and more haggard, as he called out, 'That man is loathsome. Ugh!' or, 'Do not do what you intend to do, O Man, for it will lead to your destruction!' And, again, such things as, 'That man who looks evil is to be the means of rescuing large numbers of mankind!'

His words were so confused that people thought that he must have gone mad. His face became lined as if with great age, and his beard was white, when it had been black before.

After an hour or so, the scholar wrenched himself free from the dervish's hand, and threw himself at the feet of the king. He said, 'Your Majesty, I cannot endure this knowledge one second longer. I have seen people who looked like saints, and have perceived that they were poseurs. Worse, I have seen people who thought that they were good, and their evil consisted in their thinking that they were on some good path. I have seen and felt things which no man should be expected to experience.'

The king said, 'What wisdom have you gained from this event?'

The scholar replied:

'I now understand that if anyone were to remain perceptive

to the real condition of men all the time, he would go mad.'

The dervish told him:

'Now you know that the dervish lore includes the knowledge of when to be awake and when to remain asleep.'

*   *   *

TOMORROW

Shame on you like toddlers the night before a party.
How long will you be 'one who waits for tomorrow'?

Proverb

STUPEFYING

Fair as a bride is the world. But beware—
For none may marry this stupefying one.

(Anwar-i-Suhaili)

Interpretation

A CERTAIN dervish teacher used to spend six days of each week in meditation. On the seventh, he would journey to the town nearest his Zavia and walk from one shop to another, drinking tea and holding impromptu conversations.

On one of these occasions, a stranger saw him tasting honey-cakes in company with a certain scholar. The stranger, whose knowledge of Sufism was limited to popular conceptions of the devoutness of dervishes, exclaimed aloud in the market-place:

'Shame upon the dervish who consorts with mere pedants! When a man has the choice of significant inner reflection and yet pursues childish things, he is surely far from attainment!'

Among those who heard him were some who were better informed as to the teacher's repute, but not his mode of action. They said:

'This man of knowledge is, no doubt, sharing his wisdom with mere ordinary folk; for have Sufis not always proclaimed that academics are at all times profoundly in need of converse with men of real experience.'

This thought shamed the critic. He imagined that he had learned something through what was really a shallow rebuke, based upon generalizations.

That night, however, a subtle visitant appeared to him and said:

'Because you have felt real regret, you may have a real interpretation as to the case which had perplexed you. Know, therefore, that dervishes act upon others in a manner often unsuspected by those who benefit, and unimagined by observers. The inner effect upon the scholar due to his companionship with the dervish is a thousand times greater if the dervish does not dispute with him. It is powerful even if the dervish does not speak of any matter of supposed consequence at all.

'An enlightened dervish who is silent or even talking about flies and ants is having a far greater effect upon the world than a scholar talking about theories and speculations, or a sentimentalist who thinks he has deep feelings.'

*   *   *

FIVE KINDS OF FOLLY

The Sages have said that five things are signs of foolishness:

First, seeking one's own good while harming others;

Second, looking for the yield of the last days without discipline and service;

Third, loving women harshly and brashly;

Fourth, seeking to learn the refinements of science in comfort and ease;

Fifth, expecting friendship without oneself being reliable and trustworthy.

(Anwar-i-Suhaili)

Yusuf Son of Hayula

SOLDIERS, ACCOMPANIED by a pedagogue, came to Yusuf one night, and said:

'The works of Ibn el-Arabi have been consigned to the flames this day throughout Andalusia. You have the repute of studying the Eastern Wisdom (Sufism). We shall have to take you for trial.'

'What is your warrant?' asked Yusuf.

'Our warrant is that of the Faquih Ibrahim, the jurist-scholar who stands beside you.'

Yusuf said:

'Guilt by association is not admitted by the law of God or man. I study the Eastern Wisdom, but you cannot say that I practise it.'

Ibrahim said:

'You have written three treatises on it, which are studied by young people who are indifferent to more authoritative commands.'

Yusuf said:

'The law permits anyone to study and to quote, and it does not insist that a student is a practitioner by definition.'

Ibrahim said:

'Do you deny that you practise Sufism?'

Yusuf said:

'I deny that if you bring me to trial you will be able to escape without looking a fool. When Aristotle wrote on minerals, people did not accuse him of being a mineral, and if we have come to such a state, it is time that we returned to an earlier one.'

'They could not question minerals,' said Ibrahim.

'They did not know the method.'

'You must be insane.'

'And if I am, the law will protect me, for it is forbidden to persecute the mad. The mad are under the protection of God, for they have no other natural protector, and the state must protect those who are under the protection of God.'

* * *

TASKS

Why do you let others do what should be your task?
And why, after such idleness, do you belittle others' work?

(*Anwar-i-Suhaili*)

IMPRESSIONS

Time brought a thousand impressions.
Not one of them had I seen in the mirror of the imagination.

(*Anwar-i-Suhaili*)

In China

IT IS related of a Sufi visiting China that he was approached by a group of traditionalist priests who said:

'In our country there have been sages who have interpreted the sayings of great men for many thousands of years. How then could someone come to us from outside and say or act in a manner not foreseen in our philosophy?'

He answered:

'When it is desired to bring a piece of land to fertility, the trees may have to be felled. Such an enterprise is conceived and carried out by men of wisdom. Then, perhaps when they have died, it is needful to break the soil and add to it materials which will help to support a new growth. This is carried out by people worthy of respect and admiration. When the time comes for the introduction of a perhaps formerly unknown vegetable, those who bring it are as important as those who went before in the succession; even though to an outward observer they may be outside the succession of ploughing and harrowing.

'Before the stage of the tasting of the vegetable there will assuredly be many who will say, "This is no action foreseen in our agriculture." '

*　*　*

A person is only dead when his name is not well remembered.

(*Anwar-i-Suhaili*)

To Cause Annoyance

THE SUFI master Ajnabi said:

'Write to Mulla Firoz and tell him that I have no time to engage him in correspondence, and therefore have nothing to say to his letter.''

The disciple Amini said:

'Is it your intention to annoy him with this letter?'

Ajnabi said:

'He has been annoyed by some of my writings. This annoyance has caused him to write to me. My purpose in writing the passage which angers him was to anger such as he.'

Amini said:

'And this letter will anger him further?'

Ajnabi said:

'Yes. When he was enraged at what I wrote, he did not observe his own anger, which was my intention. He thought that he was observing me, whereas he was only feeling angry. Now I write again, to arouse anger, so that he will see that he is angry. The objective is for the man to realize that my work is a mirror in which he sees himself.'

Amini said:

'The people of the ordinary world always regard those who cause anger as ill-intentioned.'

Ajnabi said:

'The child may regard the adult who tries to remove a thorn from his hand as ill-intentioned. Is that a justification for trying to prevent the child from growing up?'

Amini said:

'And if the child harbours a grudge against the adult who removes the thorn?'

Ajnabi said:

'The child does not really harbour that grudge, because something in him knows the truth.'

Amini asked him:

'But what happens if he never comes to know himself, and yet continues to imagine that others are motivated by personal feelings?'

Ajnabi said:

'If he never gets to know himself, it makes no difference as to what he thinks of other people, because he can never have any appreciation of what other people are really like.'

Amini asked:

'Is it not possible, instead of arousing anger a second time, to explain that the original writing was composed for this purpose, and to invite the Mulla to review his previous feelings?'

Ajnabi said:

'It is possible to do this, but it will have no right effect. Rather will it have an adverse effect. If you tell the man your reason he will imagine that you are excusing yourself, and this will arouse in him sentiments which are harmful only to him. Thus, by explaining you are actually acting to his detriment.'

*　　*　　*

A man's capacity is the same as his breadth of vision.

Proverb

Discouraging Visitors

A VISITOR asked Ajnabi:

'Why do you discourage people from coming to see you?'

He said:

'Because I cannot discourage them from seeing others.'

The visitor said:

'I cannot fathom this mystery. What is the meaning of such a remark?'

Ajnabi said:

' "Going to see a teacher" is in itself a condition, a state which is generally divorced from the reason for seeing a sage. If a person goes to see a teacher partly because he is in need of going to see someone, that need to go to see will act as a barrier to his understanding. That is why it is better to go to a feast and taste revelry before going to see your teacher.'

The visitor said:

'How can one discover that a visit was made for such shallow purposes as merely to visit someone?'

Ajnabi said:

'You can always tell at the departure whether the person has attained his objective. He radiates the same sensation as a man who has been to a market and gone home. Whether he has bought anything or not, he has been to a market.'

Bahaudin

ↄ৵

A TYRANT who fancied himself as a scholar wrote to Bahaudin:

'I am affronted by what you have written, which I do not regard as being historically or literally accurate.'

Bahaudin replied:

'Out of consideration for your feelings, I have written less than one-quarter of what I could have done on this subject. Consider, therefore, whether you are not in fact benefiting rather than the reverse, for I have done far less than I could have done. But know, too, that if a time comes when the welfare of my disciples requires it, I shall write the remaining three-quarters of the matter which offends you: for there is a limit to the extent to which a man may deprive them of truth out of kindness to an opinionated person, whether king, cleric or scholar.'

*   *   *

Sugar for a parrot, carrion for jackals
                    Proverb

Reading

A Sufi went to the Court of a certain king. The scholars who surrounded the throne said, 'Your Majesty, this man must not be allowed to speak until he has satisfied us that he knows in detail the classical books and commentaries, because otherwise he might harbour thoughts which could be harmful to the kingdom.'

But the Sufi could not recite any classics, and his manner of speaking was foreign to the scholars, who called him a charlatan and had him turned away.

Six months later, the Sufi appeared again and presented himself to the master of ceremonies.

'You are not allowed into the Court as a learned man, Sufi,' said the master, 'since you have failed the test.'

'But I am not here as a learned man,' said the Sufi. 'I come as one who brings a present for his Majesty.' He indicated a horse which was following him.

When he was admitted into the royal presence, the Sufi said:

'I have dared to bring this horse to Your Majesty because it has characteristics which I think worthy of a sovereign's attention.'

'And what are those?' said the king.

'Cause any volume of the classics to be brought,' said the Sufi.

As soon as the book was produced and put before the horse, it started to turn over the leaves with its hooves. From time to time it paused, looked at the Sufi, and neighed.

'Good Heavens!' said the king, 'this horse is reading the book and remarking upon passages from it.'

'Is this not even more wonderful than the capacities of the

76

scholars, who, after all, are human beings and better equipped than a horse to read books?' asked the Sufi.

'Yes, indeed,' said the king. 'But I must know how this wonder came about.'

'If I tell you, Your Majesty may be tempted to dismiss all scholars from positions of importance,' said the Sufi.

'Even at that risk, tell me,' said the king.

'Well, I trained the horse for six months by putting some oats between the pages of books,' said the Sufi, 'and that was his incentive — to earn a little for each piece that he knew. He supplied the neighing part himself.'

'But that is just the way that scholars are themselves trained.' said the king, 'so we can do without them.'

And that is the story behind the happy tale of Sufistan, the history of the future. You have heard of it, the time and place where real scholars were able to come into being because the horse-like ones and their way of training their successors and sycophants were put to flight by the king who became a Sufi.

*　　*　　*

The fruit of timidity is neither gain nor loss.

Proverb

Eyes and Light

THE CLERIC Khatib Ahmed said to Salih of Merv:

'Illuminate your abstruse subject for me, for Sufi presentations invariably remain dark when I try to approach.'

Salih of Merv observed:

'If the blind need eyes and not light, how can a brilliant presentation seem other than dark to them?'

*   *   *

TASTING

Whoever seeks only his own welfare does not taste full success.

As the timid fearing the hang-over cannot have the delights of tipsiness.

(*Anwar-i-Suhaili*)

The significance of the dwelling is in the dweller.

Proverb

Kasab of Mazar

SHEIKH KASAB of Mazar arrived at the town of Mosul and entered a mosque where a cleric was addressing a large audience on morality and good deeds.

The cleric, seeing Kasab taking his seat, called out, 'And I cannot end my remarks better than by saying that I hope that the heretic Kasab will mend his ways, and will not spread words of separation while he is among us! He will, of course, only pretend that he is speaking the truth!'

Kasab stood up and said:

'Tomorrow, in the centre of the city, I shall speak words of hypocrisy for all to hear. But those who do not wish to be corrupted may stay away, unless they are pure enough, through the constant efforts for truth exercised by this cleric, to endure my abominations.'

The following day an immense concourse of people had gathered to hear Kasab. He said:

'I have come to speak to you for your own good.'

Someone asked:

'Is this a statement of hypocrisy?'

'Yes, it is,' said Kasab, 'if it is spoken by someone who wishes only to make his name better known.'

He continued:

'I shall now make the hypocritical statement: "You must do good, because you all know what is good and what is not." '

Again someone asked him:

'How can this be a bad statement?'

'Because', said Kasab, 'people do not *know* what good is, and any intelligent man knows that. They only know what they have been told is good or bad.'

He then said:

'Words of hypocrisy include saying such things as, "Such-and-such a person is good or bad, or to be followed or to be shunned," when such words really mean "I like him or dislike him, I want to believe in him or to disbelieve him." '

Then he said:

'Does anyone want to hear further words of hypocrisy?'

There was no reply from the crowd.

* * *

SOVEREIGNTY

Sovereignty is a wind of change.

(Hariri)

The hearts of the noble are the graves of confidences.

Proverb

Satisfaction is a treasure which does not decay.

Proverb

Money

YUSUF IBN Jafar el-Amudi used to take sums of money, sometimes very large ones, from those who came to study with him.

A distinguished legist visiting him once said:

'I am enchanted and impressed by your teachings, and I am sure that you are directing your disciples in a proper manner. But it is not in accordance with tradition to take money for knowledge. Besides, the action is open to misinterpretation.'

El-Amudi said:

'I have never sold any knowledge. There is no money on earth sufficient to pay for it. As for misinterpretation, the abstaining from taking money will not prevent it, for it will find some other object.

'Rather should you know that a man who takes money may be greedy for money, or he may not. But a man who takes nothing at all is under the gravest suspicion of robbing the disciple of his soul. People who say, "I take nothing," may be found to take away the volition of their victim.'

*   *   *

As swords were designed to kill
They did well to make them tongue-shaped.

(*Anwar-i-Suhaili*)

Digestion

IBN DARANI wrote books on medicine, religion, astronomy, mathematics and the qualities of plants.

His detractors claimed that he wrote on far too many things to have profound knowledge. They added that even if he did know all these subjects, he should teach only one of them, in order to be effective.

'People become respected and authoritative', they said, 'by specializing and becoming known for one thing.'

A visitor queried Ibn Darani about this.

Ibn Darani said:

'Even a bee is known for at least two things— honey and the sting. But here is an illustration. Take this peach. If you want one thing from it, you may choose taste, colour, texture, coolness. But if you are seeking one thing in that way— you do not want a peach. Only a fool would approach a peach and say, "It has far too many things for me— why do peaches not have flavour alone?" '

*   *   *

Before the antidote arrives from Iraq
The man with snake-bite will be dead.

(*Saadi*)

82

Target

A DERVISH went to a Sufi master and said:

'Noble Guide, I wish to learn from you whatever I can communicate to others.'

The Sufi told him to go into the garden and to feed birds and animals until they came to him whenever he appeared.

The dervish did this for three years. At the end of this time he went back to the Sufi and said:

'The birds and animals come to me whenever I show myself to them.'

The Sufi said:

'Do you still want to learn in order to impart to others?'

The dervish answered:

'I have realized that I must learn whatever I can learn, and not to try to learn for a purpose until I know the value of the purpose.'

The Sufi said:

'Now you can start to learn. Unless your attention had been fixed upon the birds and animals, your real mind would not have been able to solve this problem of understanding. Attention demands an object, as an arrow demands a target. But to have an arrow in a target all the time, or to have all targets full of arrows, or to have every bowman shooting at once, or to have people thinking that shooting is necessary when they have other things which they can do and be, is evidence of stupidity and a sure road to oblivion.'

The Food of the Peacock

A Sufi sage was asked by a disciple about the behaviour of a certain dervish:

'Why did he, when he was alive, defend his reputation so strongly? Surely the Wise are unconcerned about personal matters?'

'He did so', said the Sufi, 'because he wanted to make people think, "These people are redoubtable adversaries—it is best not to cross swords with them."'

'But why should he need to gain this repute, if he was humble?'

'He did so for the purpose of preventing others, in the future, from oppression. And that is exactly what happened: many vulnerable people were preserved because oppressors and destructive thinkers feared to attack them without good cause, in case they suddenly showed the strength and resolution of the dervish of whom we speak.'

'And because he could not explain this without revealing the plan, he was assumed to be vain, self-willed and aggressive?'

'That is so. But he had no choice. He had a chance to do good for those who were to come after him, and he had to take this opportunity—whether it incurred reproach, whether it was understood or not.

Beware of making facile interpretations of the lives and sayings of the Sufis. This matter is so deep that it is really only understood by those who have arrived. Remember the saying, "If you have the stomach of an ox, do not speak of eating the food of a peacock."'

The Perfect Man

A DISCIPLE studied under a Sufi for several months. One day he said:

'Master, you are the greatest man in the world, and yet comparatively unknown. I feel that it is my duty to travel throughout the climes and tell people of your greatness. How can it be that the infinitely perfected man shall remain unknown?'

The master said:

'If I were to say that I were the infinitely perfected man, or allow anyone else to say it— you would know that I was not such a man. To feel that you must represent your teacher as the greatest man on earth is a sign of your own arrogance.'

*   *   *

The candle burned the moth:
But soon it will vanish in its own fat.
            (*Anwar-i-Suhaili*)

Yes, the world is an illusion. But Truth is always being shown there.

            (*Subhani*)

Now Begin

ALAMI SAID:

'I have said, "Read no books," and nobody reads any. But when I said that, I was saying it to an audience. Why are the instructions followed by some other audience?'

Aswad the Murid said:

'What book, then, shall I study?'

Alami told him to read the *Alamite Contemplations*.

When Aswad returned, Alami at once said to him:

'Have you read the *Contemplations*?'

'Yes,' said Aswad.

'What were my instructions to you on this matter?'

'To read the book entitled *Alamite Contemplations*.'

'Have you read the book?'

'I have read the *Contemplations*.'

'But I can tell you that you have not read the whole book.'

'I have not read the Preface, nor the Notes, because they did not seem to me to be the *Contemplations*.'

'Perhaps you would now like to begin to follow your instructions,' said Alami.

*   *   *

The bowl is warmer than the soup.

Proverb

A Thousand Dinars

JUNAID GAVE a discourse which was heard by a certain wealthy young man. This youth was so impressed that he went home and gave all he owned to the needy, except for a thousand dinars.

Taking this money, he went back to Junaid and offered it to him.

Junaid said:

'Would you seek to enmesh me in the things of the world?'

So the youth took the money up and went to a river bank. Here he threw the coins, one by one, into the water.

When he returned to Junaid to become a disciple, the master said:

'Doing something which you could do in one action in a thousand actions instead shows that you cannot become a companion of mine. Why did you not throw them all away at once?'

* * *

He has been a worker who has finished the job.

Proverb

Look at the grain of pepper — and at the size of the sneeze.

Proverb

The Ordeals

HADRAT OMAR, son of Osman of Mecca, wrote to Junaid, Shibli and Harari thus:

'Such is the terror of the Way of the Spirit that none should embark upon this journey unless he is able to ford two thousand roaring cataracts and to climb two thousand mountains belching fire. A man who is unprepared for such ordeals should abstain from calling himself a Seeker.'

Junaid said:

'I have passed through but one of these ordeals.'

Harari said:

'I have made only the first faltering steps.'

Shibli said:

'I have not seen even an indication of such terrors.'

Then a voice from beyond called out:

'Those who regard such ordeals as terrors, and who do not see them as necessary advantages, those who can dwell upon their own sufferings instead of passing through them, they are not Sufis, but something else: not people of spirit, but people of sensation. They belong to the world, and imagine that worldly feelings are sublime ones.'

*   *   *

When tomorrow comes, think tomorrow's thoughts.

Proverb

Men and Camels

BAHAUDIN NAQSHBAND was sitting on his terrace one day when a large group of would-be disciples arrived.

Their leader said:

'We have come to seek enrolment in the Teaching, and to sit at the feet of the master. May this intention find acceptance.'

Bahaudin said:

'Let everyone pass before me and say no word.'

The disciples were paraded before him.

The master then said:

'The fifth, eighteenth and thirty-fourth are acceptable for the Way.'

The leader of the disciples asked:

'May one inquire as to which characteristics indicate acceptability?'

Bahaudin said:

'What is your vocation in life?'

The man replied that he was a camel breeder.

'Then you should know the quality and potentiality of camels by seeing them pass before you. Why do you not use your own experience to tell you that a similar function might be possible to a spiritual man, working in his own sphere?'

*   *   *

Bats come out when the sun has set.

Proverb

Illustrative Exclamations

HADRAT ABUL-HASAN KHIRQANI said:

'My short-comings have been many and, comparatively, my invocations have been too few!'

A man who wanted to become a Sufi went to another master and asked him:

'What is the meaning of such a remark? If Abul-Hasan, the greatest of the saints, can say at his age that he has not done enough in one way, and has done too much in another, what hope is there for anyone who wants to learn and is of lesser rank?'

The sage answered:

'O one of bright prospects! You will not be able to enter the ranks of the elect for a long time: not because you lack the abilities of Abul-Hasan, but because you have not yet noticed that he is not referring to himself, but is acting as a mirror for your own inward self.'

*   *   *

A snake gets through the hole when it has straightened itself.

Proverb

Success in Discipleship

ଔଓଔଓଔଓଔଓଔଓଔଓଔଓଔଓଔଓଔଓଔଓଔଓଔଓଔଓଔଓଔଓଔଓ

KHAMLAT POSH said:

'I have never refused to make anyone a disciple. But most people are in reality, if not in appearance, incapable of benefiting from the phase of discipleship, so that they exclude themselves in fact from its operation.

'Discipleship is a matter of method, not potentiality. All mankind may have the makings of a higher man. Very few have learned how to approach the problem.

'Being a disciple is being able to learn, not wanting to learn alone. Nobody knows how to learn as a natural capacity—he must be given the ability.

'Desire to learn is not the basis for learning, but sincerity is. The basis of sincerity is straightforwardness and a liking for balance.

'To want to do more than you are able, and not to accept that you are not to be answered at certain times, that is failure in discipleship.'

* * *

You cannot hit two targets with one arrow.

Proverb

Pomegranates

A DISCIPLE went to the house of a Sufi physician and asked to become an apprentice in the art of medicine.

'You are impatient,' said the doctor, 'and so you will fail to observe things which you will need to learn.'

But the young man pleaded, and the Sufi agreed to accept him.

After some years the youth felt that he could exercise some of the skills which he had learnt. One day a man was walking towards the house and the doctor, looking at him in the distance, said, 'That man is ill. He needs pomegranates.'

'You have made the diagnosis—let me prescribe for him, and I will have done half the work,' said the student.

'Very well,' said the teacher, 'providing that you remember that action should also be looked at as illustration.'

As soon as the patient arrived at the doorstep, the student brought him in and said, 'You are ill. Take pomegranates.'

'Pomegranates!' shouted the patient, 'pomegranates to you —nonsense!' and he went away.

The young man asked his master what the meaning of the interchange had been.

'I will illustrate the next time we get a similar case,' said the Sufi.

Shortly afterwards the two were sitting outside the house when the master looked up briefly and saw a man approaching.

'Here is an illustration for you—a man who needs pomegranates,' he said.

The patient was brought in and the doctor said to him:

'You are a difficult and intricate case, I can see that. Let me see ... yes, you need a special diet. This must be composed of something round, with small sacs inside, naturally occurring.

An orange— that would be of the wrong colour ... lemons are too acid ... I have it: pomegranates!'

The patient went away, delighted and grateful.

'But Master,' said the student, 'why did you not say "pomegranates" straight away?'

'Because', said the Sufi, 'he needed *time* as well as pomegranates.'

∗   ∗   ∗

If you are penniless you will have a thousand dreams.
Get even a single piece of money, however, and you will have only twenty options.

Saying

Like the hawk, be a hunter and provider for others. Not an eater of scraps like the chick of a crow.

(Anwar-i-Suhaili)

The Sleeping Man

AKRAM WAS a man who earnestly sought real knowledge; and after many years he arrived at the house of a sage who knew all the secrets of life.

Akram asked for the mysteries to be revealed to him, but the wise one merely said:

'First things first, and one thing at a time.'

But after some years of attending the smallest wants of the master, Akram could only say that he had learnt that "There would be a Golden Age after several centuries."

'Then I shall travel to those future centuries,' said Akram to himself, for he could not imagine that the sage would be able to do anything for him in the meantime.

Quitting the presence of the adept, he scoured the world and eventually found someone more to his liking. This was a wonder-working fakir who agreed to put Akram into a seven-hundred-year sleep.

When he woke up, it was to find himself amid the ruins of a mighty civilization, with the remains of imposing palaces, beautiful gardens overgrown, wonders of all kinds littering the landscape.

For days Akram searched for any sign of human life. When the smoke of a small wood fire at last showed a habitation, he found beside it a wild and solitary dervish, dressed in patches.

'I seek the Golden Age,' said Akram.

'You have missed it, by two hundred years,' said the dervish.

Abdali

᠗᠗᠗᠗᠗᠗᠗᠗᠗᠗᠗᠗᠗᠗᠗᠗᠗᠗᠗᠗᠗᠗᠗᠗᠗᠗᠗

A MAN came to Abdali and said, 'I am a poor soldier, please make it possible for me to be an officer.'

A year later he wrote to say, 'I have been promoted, but I am now here fighting on the frontiers, and find it onerous; could you please help me to gain my release?'

After six months this man arrived at Abdali's Tekkia, saying, 'I am now released from the army, and have become a merchant. May I have your intercession so that I might become more prosperous?'

Abdali said:

'Alas, I cannot tell you what to do, since you are incapable of thinking any further than what you imagine to be your own interests; so you have repeatedly to apply to me for changes in your career. And you come and write to me, telling me what to do for you — and it does not benefit you.'

The man asked:

'If there is no advantage in granting my wishes, why do you do it, because everything that I have asked so far you have done for me?'

Abdali said:

'Whatever has been done for you has been done in order to show you a lesson. The lesson is: "Every time you choose an aim for yourself, it goes sour."'

The man said:

'Then choose an aim for me.'

Abdali said:

'I cannot choose an aim for you which you will fulfil properly. Your difficulty is that you are not in a condition in which you are willing to equip yourself for aims.'

The Stone

SOMEONE ASKED:

'How can a small thought be an obstacle to a great one? If a person has acquired capacities which enable him to understand important things, will these not inevitably enable him to overcome the distorting influence of small thoughts?'

Sayed Nimr said:

'Pick up stones, all of you, small ones. These stones do not block vision when they are at a certain distance: they are too small. But if you hold even the smallest stone up to your eye, it will appear large, because it will be an obstacle to vision, it will block the sight.'

* * *

There is no purpose in hammering cold iron.

Proverb

Unfettered

ᎧᏋᎧᏋᎧᏋᎧᏋᎧᏋᎧᏋᎧᏋᎧᏋᎧᏋᎧᏋᎧᏋᎧᏋᎧᏋᎧᏋᎧᏋᎧᏋᎧᏋᎧᏋ

ASKED WHAT a Sufi was, the great teacher Hadrat Nuri said:

'A Sufi is one who is himself unfettered and who is innocent, in his turn, of keeping others in bondage.

'Sufism cannot be described in terms of doctrine nor in the form of ceremonial.

'Doctrine needs coaching of a shallow kind; ritual needs repetitious practice.

'Sufism is something which is in creation, not something which is applied to the results of creation.'

*　　*　　*

The oven is hot: make bread.

Proverb

Musa of Isfahan

FOR MANY years Musa not only taught disciples but also ran the complicated affairs of his estates. On behalf of his people he argued with lawyers, sent representations to the king, and made decisions about a hundred and one day-to-day affairs.

After he died, two lawyers were talking about him. The first said:

'What an excellent illustration of how a man can be practical and also dwell in the sublime realms of thought!'

The other answered:

'Musa's life was, rather, a rare example of total teaching. His worldly actions were as important as his spiritual aspects.'

'But what could be the importance of the secular activities?'

'Twofold. First, the worldly activities enabled Musa to maintain the physical welfare of his disciples. Secondly, it enabled him to illustrate to them, every day and before their eyes, the superficiality of ordinary life.'

* * *

Sunshine proves its own existence.

Proverb

Sandals

ᏩᏋᏩᏋᏩᏋᏩᏋᏩᏋᏩᏋᏩᏋᏩᏋᏩᏋᏩᏋᏩᏋᏩᏋᏩᏋᏩᏋᏩᏋ

THE SUFI teacher Ghulam-Shah was asked what pattern he used in formulating his courses for disciples. He said:

'Barefoot until you can get sandals, sandals until you can manage boots.'

* * *

One lie will keep out forty truths.

Proverb

Struggle

A MAN once went to a dervish and spent as much time with him as he was allowed. One day, when he hoped that the time was right, he said:

'I wish to be successful in life.'

The dervish said:

'Spend two years pacing the streets of this town, crying out at intervals "All is lost!" — and then start a small shop.'

When the man eventually opened his shop, everyone in the town knew him, and most of them shunned him, because they thought that he was a crazed dervish.

Ultimately, however, the man won their confidence. His affairs began to flourish, and in due course he became unusually successful in all his undertakings.

Now, rich and powerful, he sought out the dervish who had advised him and said:

'What magic was there in your invocation of "All is lost"?'

The dervish said:

'Its value was to return you to an almost helpless condition, so that you would have to struggle so much against handicaps that you were bound to rise to the top.'

The man said:

'How did you, a man of God, learn the operation of such a material process?'

The dervish said:

'By analogy. I merely adapted the means which the spiritual man must use to the needs of the lesser world: and there was no doubt as to the outcome.'

The Yemenite Inquirer

It is related of the great Imam el-Ghazali that he was once sitting silently among a group of his students when a visitor from Yemen was announced.

When the Imam made a signal that any question might be asked, the Yemenite said:

'How are we to know you, and about you, and about your works and the meaning of your philosophy?'

The Imam gave orders for fifty different volumes of his books to be brought and presented to the visitor. He said to him:

'Study these books, and you will have the answer to your question.'

When the Yemenite had left, a disciple asked:

'I have no means of understanding the significance of this encounter. Would the Imam care to say anything about it?'

El-Ghazali said:

'You will learn through digestion of the event.'

Many years later, after the death of the Imam, someone who had heard of this interchange asked the disciple what wisdom he had acquired from it.

The disciple replied:

'I have indeed understood it, though personal laziness and superficial thinking veiled the meaning from me for a long time. The Imam was giving the Yemenite an opportunity of familiarizing himself with his teaching in the written form, so that he could eventually transcend the written form.

'The Imam knew by the questioner's behaviour and mode of approach that he had first to struggle against his bias against books.'

'But what would have happened if the questioner had con-
cluded that the Imam had specially favoured him by presenting
his books to him?'

'The Yemenite would have failed.'

'And what would have happened if the Yemenite had spent
all his time trying to torture a meaning from the fifty works?'

'No man can help such people.'

'And what would have happened if the Yemenite had been
offended by being given reading matter instead of companionship?'

'That would have shown that the Yemenite was not ready
to enter into companionship. Companionship (direct contact)
is heralded by the acceptance of the indications of the companion.'

*　　*　　*

Every stick has two ends.

Proverb

Minai's Journey

MOHSIN MINAI was unsatisfied with his conventional life as an enameller's assistant, and set off to make his fortune.

He wandered out of his native town, looking for opportunities. He had just passed the main gate when someone whom he knew slightly, called out, 'Mohsin, if you want a job as an enameller, I know someone who has a vacancy.'

Minai said, 'No thank you. I have abandoned that kind of life. I am in search of better things.'

If, however, he had taken the offer, he would soon have become a famous enameller, and a revered artist; for such was the end of the opportunity whose beginning he declined to accept.

This encounter made him all the more anxious to follow his destiny. He said to himself, 'If I had not started on my journey, and had only sat in that enameller's booth in the bazaar, I would not have been given that chance to become a fully-fledged enameller for several years. So I see that in travel there is opportunity.'

He continued on his way. Presently he met a stranger who asked him, 'What is your occupation?'

'I am a master enameller,' said Mohsin, thinking to himself, 'Well, I would have been such by now if I had stayed in my own town. Why, then, should I represent myself as only an assistant?'

The stranger said, 'My sister is getting married and I would like to give her some unique enamel article. Would you care to make it for me, if I were to give you all the materials and facilities?'

'Certainly,' said Mohsin.

So he settled down in the near-by village and made a magnificent enamelled bracelet for the wedding.

Minai said to himself:

'Here I am, making money and earning credit and admiration, by assuming a stature which I did not have before in men's eyes, but which I am manifestly able to sustain.'

He had bought a shop from the proceeds of his first large independent commission, and thought that he would spend some time in that particular town.

But, not long afterwards, someone came into the shop and said:

'I am an enameller, seeking somewhere to settle down. I would like to buy your business.' And he offered Mohsin such a very large sum of money for his shop and its goodwill that the transaction was soon completed, and Minai was on the road again.

After a day or two on his journey, Minai was attacked by brigands, who took all his money and left him stripped, beaten and helpless, by the road.

Minai did not realize that if he had stayed where he was, he would have been very much worse off, because on that very day the shop which he had sold was swallowed by an earthquake, and his successor was killed.

Minai lay there, bemoaning his fate and his lack of ability to stick to one thing, regretting his selling the shop because of greed.

Presently a charitable man passing that way approached the luckless enameller.

'Come to my house', he said, 'and I will help you.'

Minai went to his new friend's house and stayed there while his wounds healed. The man gave him a job in his garden, and Minai spent three years there, afraid to travel again in case he was unlucky and something unfortunate should happen to him. He congratulated himself, at the same time, upon his own humility in being able to suspend his ambitions and upon his capacity to fill such a humble post as gardener when he was really a craftsman. He regarded himself as specially virtuous in repaying his debt to his rescuer by serving him in exchange for such instant compassion as had been shown to a penniless wanderer.

What Minai did not know, however, was that if he had stayed there by the wayside, something completely different would have happened.

The brigands had soon quarrelled, when ill-luck struck them several times in succession. The leader was killed by his second-in-command, who brought back all Minai's money, and more as well, and threw it down on the spot where Minai had been lying, to get rid of the 'curse'.

When he had worked for a thousand days in his patron's garden, Minai begged permission to leave, and he made for the nearest town. He got himself a job as an enameller's assistant, and in due course worked his way up to the position of head enameller with a goldsmith.

'Now,' he said to himself, 'I am really back on the track again, because this is where I would have been if I had never had such ideas of greatness and had not started on my journey at all.'

But what he did not know was that his imaginings about his own humility, and his vain belief that all the events in his life formed some sort of coherent whole, were the barriers to his real progress.

When, through a misunderstanding, Minai was arrested and convicted for embezzlement, he started to rearrange his thoughts like this:

'If I had only stayed where I was I would have been better off. But such misfortunes as the present one are only trials, and I must be patient.'

What he did not realize, and never understood throughout his entire life, was that various events are part of different cause-and-effect threads in a life. Anyone who tries to put them together into one whole story flattering to himself by postulating a single destiny will meet the kind of result which is no 'test' of humility and patience at all, but a payment for his own stupidity. People who always imagine that they are under test when they are being requited, are suffering from vanity which prevents them even from imagining that at some time or other they may be reaping the harvest of something sown by them.

*   *   *

BREAD, MICE AND ...

Keep bread away from mice—and Sufi work from scholars.

Saying

The Legend of the Hidden Physician

IN A certain country there was a physician. He lived at a time when medical skill was, in most places, at a low level. He decided, because of this, to make his knowledge available in the farthest west of the continent in which he lived. In that land, called Gharb, medical knowledge was almost non-existent, though in every other way its inhabitants had developed a high culture.

Being wise as well as learned, our physician made extensive inquiries about the people of Gharb before he went there. He discovered, among other things, that there was a tendency among the Gharbs to possess themselves of anything useful that they might hear about, and use it in a destructive manner. Certain despots, again, were known to get hold of valuable facts of knowledge, and preserve them for their own private use.

He therefore caused a rumour to circulate to the effect that there was a doctor, in a far-off land, who knew the remedy to many ailments. Many people set off in search of him, mostly for the wrong reasons: for they were citizens of Gharb. Because of their eagerness (some say greed), certain of these travellers actually believed that they had found the 'wonderful doctor'. Sometimes they met him but did not know it. They then thought that their malady had been healed by some other means; sometimes they thought that their sickness had 'cured itself'.

What was really happening was that the doctor, concerned only with healing and preservation, lived incognito among his patients.

He also had representatives in other countries. These people said that they had cures for various diseases, but that they were very expensive. There was, in fact, no charge, and the medicines cost nothing at all. How, then, was the money spent?

It covered the travelling expenses of the doctor, who often had to journey personally from a great distance to examine a patient, generally without the patient's knowledge, and prescribe a course of treatment. Because, for necessary reasons, the procedure was concealed, the patients often assumed that the time taken for the medicine to work was something to do with the relationship between the body and the prescription. In reality, of course, the passage of time corresponded to the period which it took the doctor to travel to his patients.

Imagine, now, what happened when this doctor died. All the misinformed intermediaries continued to talk about the distant cure, the time and the cost. They did not know that another physician, nominated by the first, succeeded him and carried on the treatments in a way suited to changed conditions and his own individuality. He did not always choose the same representatives or their successors.

*   *   *

The repentance of the wolf is — death.

Proverb

Only Three Men in the World

ᎴᏋ

ONCE UPON a time, when the sons of Adam had multiplied exceedingly, calamities began to increase. Some of these calamities were called disease, some were called the folly of men, some were of unknown origin and meaning.

People banded themselves into tribes and nations, so that they could endure, repel or escape these calamities.

People grew apart and ceased to understand themselves and even one another. Those forms of activity which men had devised, imitated and learned, even from insects, now prevented them from giving their attention to some of the purposes for which men were originally distributed upon the earth.

The Dervish teacher Khidr travelled far and wide among the various sections of mankind, in deserts and towns, in islands and mountains, in villages and nomad camps, looking for people who might be able to hear his message: 'The real welfare of man is the same as the real welfare of men.'

But the strange fact was that there were only three men in the whole world who could hear him speak.

Khidr said to the first man, 'Come with me on a journey, for it may perhaps do you some good.'

The first man followed him, and presently they came upon a river. As they looked at it, Khidr asked, 'What would you like that river to be to you?'

The man said, 'I would like it to obey my commands, so that I could make it work for me, and that by its use I could benefit myself and also others.'

'Very well,' said Khidr.

They continued on their journey, and presently they came upon a mountain. Khidr said, 'What would you like that mountain to be to you?'

The man said, 'I would like it to give me its knowledge, for it has been here longer than I. Then I could make use of the knowledge, and pass on some of it to others.'

'Very well,' said Khidr.

They went on their way, and next they arrived at a country of smiling fields and fruit-bearing trees.

'What would you like this country to be to you?' asked Khidr.

'I would like to have this country, for I could then live here and pass my remaining years instructing others in the wisdom which I will have gained,' said the man.

'Very well,' said Khidr.

And then Khidr left this man, and in due time all these things came to pass.

Now Khidr found the second man who could hear him, and invited him to accompany him on a journey. Together they set off.

They came upon a wise man who was talking to the people, and Khidr asked the second companion:

'What would you like this man to be to you?'

'I would like him to accept me as his successor, so that when he died I could carry on his teaching,' said the second man.

'Very well,' said Khidr.

They continued on their way, and presently they came upon a gathering of men who were oppressing some innocents.

'What would you like to be able to do in these circumstances, if you had the choice?' asked Khidr.

'I would like to be able to remove this oppression from those innocents, and punish the wicked,' said the man.

'Very well,' said Khidr.

They continued on their way, and later they arrived at a town where the people had many qualities, but yet had become so narrow-minded that they would not leave the town in order to share their abilities with others.

'What would you like to be able to do about this?' Khidr asked his companion.

'I would like to be able to convince all these people that they have a duty to share what they know with everyone in the world,' said the man.

'Very well,' said Khidr. And he left this man, having granted his wishes.

Then Khidr went and found the third man, the last man in all the world who could hear him, and asked him to accompany him on a journey. The man agreed.

They had not been travelling very long when they came to a place where there were nobles and slaves, high and low and people of a middling state as well.

'What would you like to be able to do in such a situation?' asked Khidr.

'I would like to be able to do what is really right,' said the man.

'Very well,' said Khidr.

They continued on their way, and when they came to some people who were hungry, since their crops had failed, Khidr asked his companion:

'Would you like these people to be fed?'

The man answered:

'I would like them to be content with poverty when it is best for them, and discontented with it when that is right for them,' said the man.

'Very well,' said Khidr.

They continued on their journey, and presently they arrived at a place where people all appeared pious and obedient, where they maintained law and order, and where everyone seemed contented with his lot.

'What would you like to do with these people?' asked Khidr.

'I would like them to be able to understand exactly what is good for them and what they could be doing and feeling,' said the man.

'Very well,' said Khidr.

Khidr, after granting this man's three wishes, left him— and it is from these nine aspirations of the only three men in the world who could hear Khidr that every kind of human enterprise and preoccupation is derived.

It was the work of the third man, however, which found acceptance with Khidr, and which is working its way out through successive generations of men.

*   *   *

The thief who has not been caught is a king.

Proverb

The Palace of the Man in Blue

ONE DAY a group of people who had been travelling together through a certain country came upon a magnificent palace by the roadside. They stopped to admire it, and a steward came out and said:

'My master, the owner of this palace, invites you to pass a little time here. There are refreshments and diversions, if you would care to consider yourselves our guests.'

The travellers delightedly followed the man into the court-yard. Just within was a crowd of people, all watching a man in blue robes. One by one he touched the people, all of whom seemed to be ill. One by one they changed: the lame walked, the pale looked healthy again, the bent straightened.

One of the visitors said to his fellows:

'But this is the strangest thing that I have ever seen! This man is a healer, and yet, in my own town, I have seen him going from one doctor to another, seeking a cure for various ailments of his own.'

Within a few minutes the man had finished treating his patients. He dismissed them, and led the guests to a banqueting-hall where every kind of delicious food was waiting for them. As soon as they had sat down to eat, one of the company said to his neighbours:

'This is the strangest thing that I have ever seen! This man gives banquets, and yet, in my own town, I have seen him begging scraps of bread from door to door.'

When the meal was finished, the host took them to see his gardens, which covered an immense extent of land. There, amid every conceivable variety of fruit and flowers, an army of gardeners were at work, swarming like ants through the grounds.

When the man in blue was out of earshot, yet another of his guests said to the others:

'This is the strangest thing that I have ever seen! Here is a man who must employ more than five hundred gardeners. And yet, in my own locality, I have seen him desperately seeking work for himself, and often unable to find it.'

Minute by minute the wonderment of the visitors increased.

It was not diminished when yet another of them said:

'This man is well known in my own area. There, he is a beggar, piteously stretching out his hand for the smallest coin. Yet here, he must be spending more money in a day than a king does in a year.'

And, strange though it may seem, each and every one of those people had seen the man in blue, at some time or another, in circumstances of want and suffering.

When they had spent several hours in mingled enjoyment and perplexity, their host said to his steward:

'I shall retire now to rest. Please escort our friends back to the highway, and satisfy any curiosity that they might have; there may be some detail about which we have neglected to inform them. It would be against the laws of hospitality to allow them to leave us without fulfilling their desires.'

The steward took the people to the gate of the palace and they crowded around, all talking at once. One was asking about the healing, another about the food, a third about the poverty, a fourth about the expenditure of their strange host.

The steward said:

'I have one thing to say which will answer all your questions: for your questions are really all one single question, though they seem to you to be different ones. Here is your answer:

'My master, through his own self, has in the past given each and every one of you an opportunity to help him. But when a needy man asks for help and you help him, you help yourself. Thus is the way for man to do good kept open all the time, among all communities, in every possible manner.'

The steward turned and walked into the palace. As he did so, like a mirage, every vestige of it melted away.

*   *   *

No gnat stings from malice.
Proverb

The Man Who Wanted Knowledge

ᏩᏯᏩᏯᏩᏯᏩᏯᏩᏯᏩᏯᏩᏯᏩᏯᏩᏯᏩᏯᏩᏯᏩᏯᏩᏯᏩᏯᏩᏯᏩᏯ

A MAN once said to himself:

'What is the use of carrying out the observances of the order to which I am attached, of respecting the adepts, of making donations, and of reading all those books?'

A stranger who was passing by stopped, and, as if he read his mind, said:

'To each outward activity there is an inward activity. To each inward action there is an equivalent in a far-distant land.'

'But,' said the man, 'supposing people stopped following the observances of the Path?'

As if in a dream, he heard the dervish say:

'This is what would happen if there were no Sufi teachers.'

He saw that, for an instant, the water in the irrigation channels near him had dried up.

'And this is what would happen if there were no followers.'

Every piece of greenery in the countryside seemed to have turned brown and withered, in a few seconds, before their eyes.

'And this is what would happen if the right passages in the books were not being read.'

Dead birds began to fall from the skies, like hailstones.

'And this is what would happen if enough sincere people did not respect the adepts.'

The very earth started to tremble and appeared as if it was about to liquefy.

'Enough,' cried the man, 'I will obey, read, donate, go to meetings.'

'Alas,' said the dervish, as the water, the leaves and the land returned to their normal state, 'alas, you cannot now benefit through any of these promises.'

'But why?' said the man, 'for I am humbled.'

'Because you attach yourself to a teaching only through anxiety or desire. It is from such as you that the Teaching itself must detach itself.'

'But I only wanted knowledge,' said the man.

'And you got what you wanted,' said the dervish; 'something useless to you and to us.'

* * *

No problem is too difficult to be solved by a theoretician.

Proverb

The Mantle

ONCE UPON a time a traveller was shipwrecked on a remote and unvisited island.

He was dragged out of the sea half-drowned and looked after by the kindly inhabitants, who nursed him back to health.

After a time, this man began to notice something quite unusual in the local people. They had, compared to him, very short memories indeed. This made it difficult for them to store up, compare and communicate experience to one another. As a result, each generation had to learn anew: and in many cases each person had to experience the same thing again and again before he could profit by experience at all.

The traveller also noticed that, if he wore the mantle which had been wrapped around him when he arrived, this served to maintain his own memory: otherwise it became weaker and weaker.

He realized that the garment in some way counteracted the local climate which was responsible for causing amnesia and maintaining it.

So this mantle became, as it were, the stranger's robe of distinction. People respected him mainly because of his memory. He started to manufacture these robes and tried to get the people to wear them. It was, however, against their customs, and many were opposed to wearing them because they associated them with the great 'power' and superiority of their visitor.

He was, however, able to induce some people to wear the robes. They, providing that they made the often forgotten effort to remember, found themselves now endowed with memories.

The majority of the people continued to wear no robe, or

else to affect them without making the necessary efforts, and in time all that was effectively left of the knowledge and its application was the phrase, in the language of that people, 'to assume the mantle' or 'to be invested with a robe', denoting distinction and authority.

Like all people everywhere, the people had confused distinction and authority, elegance and prestige, with that which underlies it— capacity.

That island is still there. So are its people. The traveller has passed on his way.

The robes continue to perform the decorative, ritualistic and emotion-arousing functions which the people now regard as appropriate to them.

*　　*　　*

Sleeping is to hunters as excitement is to students.

Proverb

Unwritten History

IBRAHIM YAKUBOV had a small shop. He was not a popular man, because he did not spend time with other people, and nobody knew very much about him.

Nobody knew what he did in his house, and everyone wanted to know. Nobody knew what he thought and felt about the things which interested them. All the other people in his town spent their time talking about what they thought and felt.

When Yakubov died, they found in his house a beautiful carpet which he had been weaving.

'He couldn't have made this, for that man had no soul,' said the people.

Then, one day, a 'man with a soul' appeared, and everyone fell under his spell. And in the end he destroyed them: just because they had decided that those whom they called 'people with souls' were good, and that others were bad.

*   *   *

If you cannot lie down, you will stand up once too often.

Proverb

The Legend of the Cattleman

‿‿‿‿‿‿‿‿‿‿‿‿‿‿‿‿‿‿‿‿‿‿‿‿‿‿‿‿‿

THERE WAS once a cattleman, who travelled far from his homeland in order to earn his living and also to share his special skill and knowledge with the cattle-raisers of other lands.

When he arrived in the country where he had decided to settle, he gave himself out as a cattle expert. At first people crowded around him, anxious to learn his knowledge.

They said:

'We welcome you, for we are specialists in cows and oxen, and we need such as you, although this is not a good country for raising such animals, as they become sick and die very frequently, in spite of all our science.'

He asked them:

'And how do you feed and treat your animals?'

They described their methods to him, and he at once saw that because of deep but false imaginings about the nature and treatment of cattle, they were actually preventing their own herds from multiplying and even from flourishing.

To them, their own feelings were more necessary than the proper raising of cattle, though they imagined that they were serving their herds.

When he tried to point this out to them, they displayed such horror and dismay that he was compelled to say, 'I am only jesting; of course you are right in the way in which you treat your animals.'

Because he had said that, the people allowed him to work with their animals. They appointed him in the end to be their main administrator of cattle.

This meant that this man had employment in the country of his choice. But when it came to the matter of being able to carry out his principal ability—that of tending and treating cattle—his condition was one of great anxiety and trouble for him.

Because he was compelled by local requirements to treat the cattle with famous but useless remedies when they were sick, he had to spend one-third of his nights, when he could have rested, in making the rounds of the herds and administering the right curatives to them.

Because he had to feed the cattle with insufficient nutrients, since these were the ones which the local people considered right, he had to spend another third of his free time in secretly feeding to the cattle what they really needed.

Only one-third of the necessary allotment of rest ever remained to him.

His life was shortened by this way of living, but he attained high repute among the cattle-people, who regarded him as a paragon of the virtues in cattle-wisdom which was enshrined in their own previous history and aspirations.

The cattle herds improved and flourished. When he died and the puzzled cattle-people tried to redouble what they imagined to be correct formulas for dealing with their herds, the animals died even more often than they had done before they had ever known the newcomer.

It was only because he left a son sworn to secrecy, who eventually took his father's place, that the people's welfare, and that of their cows and oxen, was, in spite of themselves, maintained.

*　*　*

The best player of a game is the watcher—ask him.

Proverb

The Handicap

A PERSIAN carpet-weaver challenged a Turkish weaving master to a contest.

Each was to make the best carpet that he could, so that a panel of judges might finally decide who was the greatest weaver in the world.

But the Turk was a philosopher whose teaching for many years had been summed up in this phrase:

'Never refuse, but never contend.'

So he accepted the challenge, saying only:

'I must make one proviso, because of the known disparity between your work and mine.'

'Yes, indeed,' said the Persian, 'I am prepared to agree to a handicap.'

'Very well,' said the Turkish master, 'the condition shall be that I give you a start of twelve thousand years.'

*   *   *

Be a tiger—if you are ready for a tiger's problems.

Proverb

How Things Work

THERE WAS a venerable dervish, who, being able to ignore certain anxieties due to the degree of his development, was much respected by the local people.

One day they made a collection and presented him with a sheep, which he took to his retreat, and looked after carefully.

A thief, however, heard that the old man had a sheep, and decided to steal it. He started along the road towards the dervish's abode.

On the way, he met a devil, and asked him where he was going. 'As a matter of fact,' said the devil, 'I'm on my way to the cave of such-and-such a dervish. He is interfering with the customary operation of human weaknesses, and I have decided to kill him.'

'We have no real diversity of aims,' said the thief, 'for I am going to the same dervish's place. My mission is to steal his sheep.'

So they walked on in silence and amity for some time.

Presently the devil began to think, 'If I let the thief steal the sheep first, he may alert the dervish, whom I need to surprise when he is asleep.'

The thief, for his part, was thinking at the very same time, 'If I let this devil get to the dervish first, he may cause such a commotion that the people of the neighbourhood could be aroused. They might prevent me getting the sheep, and my night would be wasted.'

When they arrived outside the dervish's cavern, the devil said, 'Let me go in first, then I can kill the man and you can walk in and carry away the sheep.'

'No,' said the thief, 'let me go in first and get the sheep. I can tell you if he is awake or not.'

They started to argue, and then to exchange blows, and finally to scream at each other so loudly that the dervish came to the cave-mouth to see what was going on.

At the sight of him the devil, overcome with hatred for the thief, shouted out, 'Look out, dervish! This is a thief, and he's going to steal your sheep.'

The thief, furious with the devil and affronted by his impudence, screamed, 'This is a devil, and he's going to kill you!'

As the dervish stood there, everyone in the neighbourhood, wakened by the din, came pouring from their houses and surrounded the fighting pair. They were given such a buffeting that they fled; and neither a thief nor a devil has been seen in that locality for centuries.

*   *   *

No hungry fish ever refuses to eat another.

Proverb

Three Villages

THERE WAS once a wise man. He divided his time between three villages.

In the first village, he gave instruction to groups of people, one party at a time. He told them and showed them things, and gave them observances to perform.

He used to spend a great deal of time away from this village. The result was that the villagers split into even smaller groups. Some of them believed that he would come back, others felt neglected. Some of them invented their own teachings, and some of them made use of his name to influence fellow-villagers. Many of them weakened in resolution because of his absences.

There was a second village. The wise man used to spend most of his time there, and people came to visit him, and attended his contemplation-hall regularly. These people sang his praises and always seemed to do what he asked, and believed that they were in harmony with him and with each other.

One day the wise man went to a third village. Taking some pupils from there, he showed them each village in turn.

'The first village is in the condition in which we saw it because you have not given enough attention to its people— you must nurse them,' said the newcomers, thinking that they had understood his point. 'Look how well behaved the people are where you spend so much more of your time,' they continued.

The wise man answered them, 'On the contrary. You have to leave people alone from time to time, so that you and they can see what they are really worth. The pot is stirred in order to mix: but also in order to produce the scum and the dregs. If you spend all your time with people, they become accustomed to you, and they have no self-reliance in your absence, as in the first village; whereas, as in the second, their self-reliance is invisible, because it is never tested.'

'Then', asked the observers, 'which is the better method?'

'Neither. Each is an incomplete part of a total method. In order to produce learning, you must have those who are frequently seen to mix with those who are seen sometimes. And a few of those who— like you— are prone to misinterpret, may be included as well.'

* * *

If you want to know what he's like— reverse what his opponents say.

Proverb

The Sutra of Neglectfulness

It is the duty of Khidr, the Hidden Guide, to travel about the earth in various guises, in different ages, provoking a state of mind in man, such that he shall have a chance to gather his scattered self.

There were once three men whom Khidr had to test.

The first one was suffering from a terrible disease, and Khidr went to him. He said, 'What do you want?'

The man said, 'I want relief from this distress.'

'And what else?'

'I would like money, so that I may flourish in the world.' Khidr gave him both wishes.

Then he heard the supplications of a second man. He went to him and said, 'What do you want?' The second man said:

'I want only that my friend and adviser, who is being tortured, should be released, for he is near to death because of his enemies.'

'And what else do you want?'

'I want that I should have property, so that I may have the respect of men.' Khidr gave him both of his wishes.

Then Khidr went to the third man, who wanted something very badly. 'What do you want?' he asked him.

'I want protection for my children, for they are in fear and terror.'

'And what else do you want?'

'I want importance, so that men shall respect me and make my life easy.' Khidr granted these wishes.

Some time later, however, he visited the three men again to see what they had made of their lives, and how they were living them. To the first he appeared in disguise, and said:

'I am a poor traveller, and I need some help, some money,

to reach my destination. The way is long, and I have no recourse other than you.'

'Am I a banker?' asked the first man; for he had made himself forget the days when he was needy himself. 'I can give you nothing-- unless you can help me, because in the past few years, although I have money, I have become lame in one foot.'

'Do you not remember me?' asked Khidr.

'No,' said the man, 'I do not remember you. Be off!'

Then Khidr went to the second man, who was in a flourishing condition. 'I am a poor traveller,' he said to him, 'and I need your help, for many are dependent upon me, and I must reach my destination, so that I can help them by my work when I get there.'

'But you are not a member of my community,' said the second man. 'And I can help only those who adhere to my laws. Why should I help you?' So Khidr went on his way.

He arrived at the door of the third man, and said, 'You may have forgotten me. One day I helped you, when you wanted protection for your children, and also to become respected by men, so that you could flourish.'

The man looked at him for a long time. 'I have no memory of such a transaction,' he said, for he had forgotten it; 'but I will help you, for I do not think that I should always give something away only in payment of a debt or in expectation of gain for myself.'

A superficial and sanctimonious theoretician of the Sufi lore who was present turned on Khidr and abused him roundly. 'This friend of mine is clearly a saint,' he said, 'and his words should make you ashamed of yourself, trying to manipulate his feelings!'

Remedy

A CERTAIN dervish spent many years in perfecting a remedy for the illness of a man who happened to be rich. So excited was he by the success of the preparation that he set off to carry it to the patient without consulting his Sufi mentor, to see whether circumstances had changed. On the way, however, he met another man in a caravanserai, and told him the formula and the wonderful effects of his discovery.

As soon as he was asleep for the night, this villain stole the medicine, substituted sugared pomegranate juice, and hastened ahead to cure the sick man, hoping for a reward.

The villain gave some of the medicine to the rich man, but it immediately made him worse. And the thief crept away, convinced that the dervish was mad and that his remedy was useless. And so even his knowledge of the recipe was of no value to him. He even felt relieved that he had not been found out, and that the patient's servants had not beaten him as a charlatan.

When the dervish arrived at the patient's bedside and gave him pomegranate juice — it cured him with one mouthful.

*　　*　　*

If one drop falls, why not two?
Saying

In the Land of Fools

ONCE UPON a time there was a man who strayed from his own country into the world known as the Land of Fools.

He soon saw a number of people flying in terror from a field where they had been trying to reap wheat. 'There is a monster in that field,' they told him. He looked, and saw that it was a water-melon.

He offered to kill the 'monster' for them. When he had cut the melon from its stalk, he took a slice and began to eat it. The people became even more terrified of him than they had been of the melon. They drove him away with pitchforks, crying, 'He will kill us, next, unless we get rid of him.'

It so happened that at another time another man also wandered into the Land of Fools, and the same thing started to happen to him. But, instead of offering to help them with the 'monster', he agreed with them that it must be dangerous, and by tiptoeing away from it with them he gained their confidence. He spent a long time with them, in their houses, until he could teach them, little by little, the basic facts which would enable them not only to lose their fears of melons, but even to cultivate the fruit themselves.

* * *

If it is dark enough, one candle is plenty.

Saying

Cooking the Cabbage

Two THIEVES met one day in the Land of Fools.

As with all people of the same profession, they started to boast of their exploits.

One of the thieves said:

'I once stole a cabbage as big as a house!'

The other said:

'*I* once stole a saucepan as big as a palace.'

The first thief said:

'What would anyone want a thing like that for?'

Said the second thief:

'It was needed to cook your cabbage in!'

* * *

The scorpion doesn't look much—in between stings!

Saying

The Branch

ONCE UPON a time, in the Land of Fools, a stranger to the country found that the branch of a tree had broken and was about to destroy a dam full of water.

He seized the branch and held on to it. Soon afterwards a party of people of the Land of Fools came walking by.

They said:

'What are you doing with that branch?'

He answered:

'How lucky you have arrived! Help me to lift this branch, for otherwise the dam will be broken, and we shall all die.'

They laughed and laughed. Finally the wisest among them said:

'Dear friends! This is a delicious moment: savour it. Not only does this man, talking about a branch, imagine that we are stupid enough to think that it has some relevance to a dam — but he imagines that by relating it to an ancient fear of ours he will make us obey him!'

And so, in paroxysms of laughter, the people of the Land of Fools went on their way.

The end of the story is exactly what you think it is.

*   *   *

If you see a writer who has his own pen — he isn't one.

Saying

The Fruit

ᘓᘓᘓᘓᘓᘓᘓᘓᘓᘓᘓᘓᘓᘓᘓᘓᘓᘓᘓᘓᘓᘓᘓᘓᘓᘓᘓᘓ

IT WAS reported to the Very Wisest Men of the Land of Fools that the trees were bearing, and so they went out to collect fruit.

The trees, sure enough, were laden, their branches pulled down almost to the ground.

When the Very Wisest Men reached the trees, they fell to discussing which crop they would harvest first. Since they could not come to any agreement on this, they tried another subject. Now they discovered that there was no accord about whether to pluck the fruit with their left or right hands. Then there was another problem of equal difficulty; and another, until they realized that they must withdraw to a more suitable place to thrash things out.

Finally, after full participation of all the learned institutions, all was settled. The Very Wisest Men again found themselves under the trees. But by then it was winter. The fruit had fallen and lay rotting on the ground.

'What a pity that these trees are so treacherous,' exclaimed the Very Wisest Men. 'Those branches had no right to swing up again like that. But never mind: you can at least see that the fruit was rotten anyway.'

*   *   *

Even a cup of tea, if you drink it, will force you to 'answer' it.

Saying

The Magic Word

⊙⅋

THE THREE Wisest Men of the Land of Fools, by some lucky chance, met Khidr, walking the Earth trying to impart wisdom.

'Would you like to know the Word whereby everything can be accomplished?' he asked them.

'Yes, indeed,' said the Three Wise Men.

Khidr said:

'Are you ready to hear it?'

'Yes, indeed,' said they.

So Khidr told them the Word.

The First Wise Man said:

'But this is a word which anyone could pronounce— this cannot be of any use.' So he promptly forgot it.

The Second Wise Man said:

'This word is too inelegant for me,' and he found that he could not remember it.

The Third Wise Man said:

'It can be written down— so it cannot be of any use. It does not sound like what I expected— so it is not the right *kind* of Magic Word.'

Then they all noticed that a deputation of ordinary citizens of the Land of Fools was waiting to hear some of their wisdom, so they hurried off to fulfil their obligations.

How To Prove It

⊗⊗⊗⊗⊗⊗⊗⊗⊗⊗⊗⊗⊗⊗⊗⊗⊗⊗⊗⊗⊗⊗⊗⊗⊗⊗⊗

TWO PEOPLE of the Land of Fools were talking.
The first said:
'I'm no idiot, I can multiply numbers!'
The second said:
'I don't believe it!'
'I bet you this silver coin that I can,' said the first.
'Go ahead then, let's hear you,' said the second.
'Here you are,' said the first man. 'Two and two are ninety-nine!'
'Fair enough, here's your money!'

*   *   *

People make a hat out of a pair of shoes and then wonder why you ask them why they are not walking on their heads.

Saying

Yearning

ᘛᘚᘛᘚᘛᘚᘛᘚᘛᘚᘛᘚᘛᘚᘛᘚᘛᘚᘛᘚᘛᘚᘛᘚᘛᘚᘛᘚᘛᘚᘛᘚᘛᘚᘛᘚ

A MAN said to the sage Humayuni:

'In my earlier years, I used to yearn for a teacher and for instruction. But I never found any which fully satisfied me, and now I no longer feel such a need.'

Humayuni said:

'If you had sought a teacher and a teaching, being content with what you found, you would have been a Seeker. In fact, while you were only seeking the fulfilment of a yearning, you were unteachable at the time. The thirsty man may be incapable of recognizing water if over-thirstiness has maddened him.

'The way to find water is not always to increase your thirst. It depends upon the degree and nature of the thirst at the right moment.'

*   *   *

A camel is dear at twopence if you have not got twopence.

Proverb

Man and Sufi

IT IS related that someone once said to Mulla Jami:

'You do not behave like a great poet and Sufi: how do we know that you are genuine?'

He replied:

'*You*, on the other hand, behave almost exactly like a human being — that is how we know that you are not yet one!'

* * *

The cat can do what the tiger can not.

Proverb

The Book

A YOUNG man was about to be married, and his prospective father-in-law was an unbearably pious and literal-minded cleric.

The youth went to his Sufi mentor and asked how the old man might be directed towards the Path of Understanding.

'He will be directed,' said the sage.

'But in what manner?'

'The question has been formulated, the answer will develop, the question is not permissible,' said the Sufi.

'Then how should I act towards my father-in-law, if that is a legitimate question?' asked the bridgeroom.

'Put up with him.'

When the wedding day came and the couple moved into their new home, the cleric followed them, bearing on his back a huge leather-bound box. On its cover was inscribed: 'The Holy Recital'.

The newlyweds put the case on a shelf and left it there.

Some months later things went wrong for the young man. He lost his job, his small capital was soon exhausted, and he thought about approaching his moneyed father-in-law for help to set himself up in a small business and to meet his growing debts.

'Approach your father-in-law by all means,' counselled the Sufi sage.

The young man wrote a letter outlining his situation to his wife's father, and the old man arrived in short order, bringing with him the local judge and a couple of other scholars.

When all were assembled in the sitting-room, the old man quavered:

'You have been brought to this pass through your own flagrant disregard for the *Sharia*, the Sacred Law.' So saying, he pointed to the Koran-case, and called for it to be brought down and opened.

'But why should you say that we do not have regard for the Law?' asked the young man.

'You do not read the scriptures,' said the cleric. Sure enough, when the box was opened, it was found to be filled with gold pieces.

Then the young man said, 'But has it not been said that "Knowledge is better than reading"?'. And he explained that he knew the Koran by heart.

The judge said, 'You brought me here in order to pronounce whether this young couple were pious or not. I certainly cannot say that you can find fault with this son-in-law of yours.'

'No indeed,' said the ancient, 'and I do sincerely repent, for this youth, modestly refraining from having made any play of his erudition before this time, has shown me that he is a better scholar than I am, both in conduct and in knowledge. I acknowledge myself to be outdone, and henceforth I shall strive to learn the Koran by heart.'

The two scholars exclaimed, 'How excellent is his humility, and how admirable his resolve to perfect his erudition!'

'But', said the judge, 'it has also been said that "Public humility ceases to be so when it is the subject of dramatic show."'

'Yet what is better than following the example of one who does not simply read the Koran, but has gone to the trouble to learn it by heart?' asked the ancient.

'Because public drama is destructive to real achievement, I shall tell you privately,' said the judge.

And what he told the academic made him exclaim:

'This has saved me from becoming one learned from books: I will henceforth follow the path of the Sufis, the people of practice and being.'

And he became a Sufi, whose life illuminated, and still suffuses, the thoughts and deeds of the People of the Way.

What the judge had told him was:

'You and your fellow intellectuals read the Koran. The young man knows it by heart. But your daughter, his wife: she thinks and lives in accordance with it, although she can neither read nor write, nor dispute, nor recite.'

* * *

Nobody comes to the home of a dervish asking for land-tax and house levies.

Saadi

Dervishood

ABUL HASAN insisted:

'Thinking about the affairs of this world is nothing to do with the matter of the dervish path.

'Thinking about the next world is nothing to do with the matter of the dervish path.

'They stand in relation to one another as yesterday does to tomorrow.

'Today— something similar but having its own individuality — that is the dervish path.'

* * *

A solved problem is as useful to a man's mind as a broken sword on a battlefield.

Proverb

The Reflection Chamber at
Doshambe

THE MANNER of tiling of the walls of the reflection chamber of Doshambe was thus:

Hamid Parsa asked his disciples, some of them tile-craftsmen, to arrange for the chamber (Dar el Fikr) to be tiled.

They made a start on the work, and then it was delayed by a variety of obstacles.

Hamid Parsa made inquiries from time to time, and in the end the master craftsman said:

'O Pathfinder (Rahnuma) we have not enough men and we have not succeeded in tiling the walls and we think it would be better to say this now, since such a long time has elapsed, and you may probably wish to make other arrangements so that the chamber shall be completed for whatever use you desire it.'

Hamid Parsa answered:

'Very well. Leave this work, and I will arrange for its completion.'

The craftsmen were assigned to other tasks. After two years Hamid Parsa called them in and showed them that the walls were impeccably tiled with glazes and workmanship of the highest quality and astonishing beauty.

After Hamid died, it was discovered that his frequent absences from the Tekkia were due to his having spent his time in a tile-yard, where he had made the necessary tiles himself. Later he had fixed them in the walls, without mentioning this to anyone except certain assistants whom he asked to say nothing about the matter.

His successor, Miran Jan, was asked:

'Why did the Pathfinder not tell us that he had done this work himself?'

Miran answered:

'His explanation to me was that if he told you, you would feel rebuked, and that you were not in a condition in which rebukes were useful. Or, he said, "They would in laziness, masquerading as proper admiration, regard me as some kind of wonder. Their trouble is laziness, my need was for the tiling. So I worked on the tiling and I gave them work to do to improve their condition of laziness." '

* * *

There is one kind of man worse than a boastful man: a complaining one.

Proverb

Learning of the Unripe

A MAN came to Khwaja Ahrar ('Master of the Free') and asked him a question.

When the Khwaja had given him the reply, he asked permission to go, and at once quitted the assembly.

Ahrar said:

'He was wise to ask the question.'

Allama Sadrudin said:

'Did he know why he asked it?'

'He did not know, but a part of him knew.'

Sheikh Mustafa Najur said:

'He was also wise enough to leave as soon as he had the required information.'

Ahrar replied:

'Yet that was another part of him. He was thinking that he should start off in time for congregational prayers in the Great Mosque.'

Haidar Gul inquired:

'Can a man then be wise inwardly, in some part of himself, when he is generally under the impression that he is unripe?'

'Were it not so, no man could attain wisdom in its fullness,' said the Master Ahrar.

Alacrity and Respect

MUSA FARAWANI said:

'I served Sharif Abdalmalik for twenty years, and all I got from him was indifference. But I persevered, hoping that I would understand why he should pay so little attention to me. But I have never been able to solve this mystery.'

Daud, son of Zulfi, answered:

'Did you serve him with the same alacrity which you would have shown had he been the king?'

'I suppose not.'

'Did you serve him as faithfully as one serves the making of a complicated object, as does an artisan?'

'I suppose not.'

'Did you serve him with the alacrity which you would have shown if he had been a high official or a military commander, if you had been a petty official or a mere soldier?'

'I suppose not.'

'Then he was waiting for you to manifest those forms of service. The Sharif, himself serving something of the very highest, could not accept any service less than that which is manifested in lower concerns.

'You call something a "mystery" when you will not see it. You call something service which is not service at all. You have not yet begun to serve, therefore you cannot ask why your non-existent "service" has not been accepted.'

The Cripples

IN A public square one day, some people were shouting:

'Down with the Throne!'

They were faced by a party of Royal Guards, who were trying to beat them and take them prisoner.

Sufi Zafrandoz, accompanied by a few students, was watching the scene.

'Which party should we aid?' asked a pupil.

'The cripples!' said Zafrandoz.

'Which are the cripples?'

'Both. The one party is incapable of ceasing to oppose authority. The other is unable to cease opposing them.

'People handicapped in such a manner are in the grip of a disability which hampers them. They are crippled in thought as surely as a lame man is crippled in body. Why, therefore, do we feel sorry for, and try to help, only the physically handicapped, who are such a minority?'

Names

ௐௐௐௐௐௐௐௐௐௐௐௐௐௐௐௐௐௐௐௐௐௐௐ

ANWAR OF NISHAPUR was asked:
  'Tell us one kind of Sufi whom we should avoid.'
  He said:
  'You cannot avoid any real Sufi. But if you want to avoid people, then avoid those who themselves use titles like 'murshid' (guide) and who do not leave it to others to address them thus.'

*   *   *

There are people with dyed hair who fear that it might affect the brain. But often such people have no brains.

Proverb

Repetition

A FOOLISH man came to Abdullah Manazil and asked him a question. Manazil answered, and at the end of the discourse, the man said:

'Please say that again.'

Manazil said:

'You asked me a question and I was ill-advised enough to expect that you would understand the answer. Now you have asked me to repeat my mistake.'

*   *   *

I saw a man drowning in the Jihun River—he was, I think, from Samarkand—crying and shouting, 'Alas, my cap and turban!'

Saadi

Bricks and Walls

THEY ASKED Minai:

'What are we to make of the work of the teachers of the past? We read their books and the accounts of their doings and sayings recorded for us. We perform their exercises, and we visit the places of their burial and teaching. Some people say, "Do not visit shrines"; others say, "Do not read books." '

Minai answered:

'The similitude of this situation is as the similitude of a strong wall built in the past. The old teachers are the original masons and the present teachers are the working masons. The disciples are like the populace, for whose protection the masons worked.

'The masons built walls, shall we say, to define certain limits. Those limits are there still, in some cases. In other cases the boundaries have changed. The present masons fix the boundaries again. In the same way, walls were formerly built for protection of the people. The climates and winds may have changed, or the people may have changed. They look at the wall, and wonder how it may shelter them. But this old wall will not now do so.

'Consequently the present masons take the bricks, and make suitable walls for the people of the time. The books are bricks. Some masons ask you to read certain books. This is their instruction, for they can show you what wall to build. Some say, "Do not read books" because they mean, "This is not the wall we have to build"; or even, "We have not got to the stage of building a wall." '

The Hole and the Thread

A CERTAIN great Sufi was asked about the role and status of some of his predecessors.

He said:

'To erect a small building you may first have to excavate a large hole.

'To make a large carpet you may have to start with a single thread.

'When you can see the building or the carpet, your question is answered.

'But when your question is about the hole in the ground and the thread in the hand, you can only be answered in this parable.'

*　　*　　*

It is *my* hand, and it is *my* mouth.

Proverb

The Squirrel

MAULANA BAHAUDIN was walking along a grassy bank with Alaudin of Nishapur.

Alaudin said to him:

'I wish to know why it is that you have taken away from people the enjoyment of so many habits in Sufism. You may be right, and I will be the first to agree that you probably are, in saying that such practices are trivial. But you leave the people with nothing if you do not allow their companionship to become a source of joy for them.'

Bahaudin said:

'There is a scene unfolding before us. Watch it and you will have your answer, if you can understand it, esteemed up-holder of legitimate pleasures.'

In front of the pair several small boys were playing. They were throwing, from hand to hand, a squirrel which they had caught, and whose feet they had bound together. As they ran here and there, they roared with laughter, excitement and pleasure on every face.

After a few moments an older youth, seeing what they were doing, ran up to them from the roadside. He took the animal and removed the cord from its paws, and let it go. The players of the squirrel-game were furiously angry now, and they shouted all kinds of abuse at the older boy.

Alaudin says:

'Had it not been for this demonstration, I am sure that I would never have realized the relative situation and concealed dangers in what we assume to be legitimate pleasure. But ever since then, throughout my life, I have often found that what appears to be desirable is being done at the expense of some-thing else; and that what pleases people, even "sincere" people, can be found to be making an appetite for an unsuspected vice.'

*   *   *

If you want to know who is the bravest among cowards: it is the one who first dares to kick the fallen lion.

Saying

Behaviour

ARIF OF Damascus was asked:
'How many ways are there of behaving towards visitors?'
He said:
'Two. The first is the behaviour which makes people want
to stay with you. The second is the behaviour which makes
them want to go away. There is no behaviour which conveys
anything more than this, friendship or hostility, known to
people, apart from those who no longer need it.'

*　　*　　*

MUD

The false student is the one whose eyes are fixed upon
heaven because his feet are planted in mud.

Saying

Bahaudin Naqshband said:

ᏬᏬᏬᏬᏬᏬᏬᏬᏬᏬᏬᏬᏬᏬᏬᏬᏬᏬᏬᏬᏬ

MANY THINGS are invisible to people because of the unexpectedness of where they really are. Who would expect silk to come from worms?

People imagine that because they have grasped this point, they can exercise expectation. But, expectation may conceal the visibility of something by obsessing the observing person.

Unexpectedness is a form of expectation: 'I did not expect that' means 'I was expecting something else.'

Expectation alone is useless. The expector must be informed.

* * *

What is known to be tyranny to the superior man may appear to be justice to the ordinary one.

Proverb

Genealogy

A HAUGHTY aristocrat fell into a well, and hung suspended just above the water, praying and shouting for help.

After some time another man came along and said:

'Take my hand, and I will pull you out.'

'One moment,' said the trapped man, reverting to habit, 'I must first know your name.'

'My name, if it is of any importance, is Omar, son of Zaid, of the Tribe of Hashim.'

'Of course it is of importance,' said the nobleman, taking his hand, 'but I must know whether you trace your descent through Ali Raza or Musa Kazim.'

'Well if you must, you must. I'll go and look it up,' said Omar. He let go of the hand and returned home to consult his pedigree.

When he got back the other man had drowned.

One of Ours

༄༅༄༅༄༅༄༅༄༅༄༅༄༅༄༅༄༅༄༅༄༅༄༅༄༅༄༅༄༅

A THEOLOGIAN found himself at the entrance to the Gardens of Paradise. He had a pious look, and the angel on duty asked him a nominal question or two and then said:

'Pass, friend, enter the Garden.'

'Not so fast, my boy,' said the cleric; 'I am a noted Believer, impeccable in faith and renowned for my intellect, accustomed to making up my own mind, and not to people making up their minds about me. How can you prove that this *is* Paradise, and not a snare and a delusion: think carefully before you answer.'

The angel rang a bell and angelic guards appeared.

'Take this one inside, will you? He's one of ours all right.'

*   *   *

Learn how much knowledge is needed before we can see how ignorant we are.

Proverb

Three Reasons

THERE WAS once a powerful conqueror who had become emperor of a vast territory peopled by representatives of several beliefs.

His counsellors said, 'Great king, a deputation of thinkers and priests from each persuasion is awaiting audience. Each hopes to convert you to the way of thinking of his school. We are in a quandary, because we cannot advise you to accept the ideology of one party, since it would alienate the goodwill of all the rest.'

The king, for his part, said, 'Neither is it fitting that a king should adopt beliefs for political reasons, and without thought for his own higher dignity and well-being.'

The discussions continued for several hours, until a wise dervish, who had attached himself to the king's retinue many months before and had been silent ever since, stepped forward.

'Majesty,' he said, 'I am prepared to advise a course in which the interests of all parties will be safeguarded. The applicants will be abashed, the courtiers will be relieved of their anxiety to find a solution, the king will be able to retain his reputation for wisdom, and nobody will be able to say that he holds sway over the king's thoughts.'

The dervish whispered his formula into the royal ear, and the king called the deputation to enter the throne-room.

Receiving the clerics and thinkers with all courtesy, the king said to them:

'I shall hear first of all the arguments of those among you who do not say "Believe or you are in peril"; or "Believe because it will give you happiness", or "Adopt my beliefs because you are a great king."'

The applicants dispersed in confusion.

Exile

IMADUDIN SHIRAZI was ordered to leave Persia for maintaining that certain ancient poets were Sufis, contrary to the beliefs of scholars who had influenced the Shah.

He sent a letter to the king:

'Your Majesty's order is accepted with all obedience. This insignificant person will leave the Imperial domain for ever. I am honoured by being noticed, even, by one whose power is greater than that of God.'

The Shah called him to explain his heresy.

'The Shah can send me out of his realm, into exile,' Shirazi said; 'but God, Ruler of the Universe, cannot banish a man beyond his own jurisdiction. Anyone who can banish people has powers which exceed God's.'

* * *

Since when did a tiger go a-mousing?

Proverb

The Medicine

A SUFI teacher on his death-bed gave a bundle of papers to his disciple and said:

'Take these. Some are written upon and others not. Those which are blank are as valuable as those which are not.'

The disciple took the papers, and studied those on which there was writing. The others he kept just as carefully, waiting until their value might be vouchsafed.

One day he was lying in a caravanserai, ill and shuddering with a fever, and a doctor was called, as he seemed on the point of death.

The doctor said:

'We have no time to lose. Find a piece of paper, of fine quality, upon which I may write a talisman for the relief of his malady.'

The other people present looked all around. Searching the traveller's knapsack they came upon some blank sheets in the bundle of writings of the Sufi teacher.

The physician tore up a sheet, and on it he inscribed a strange figure. 'Steep this in water. When the ink has dissolved, give it to the patient, and he will be well in three hours,' he said.

They did as he directed, and the disciple was soon cured. The effect had been due to a medicament which had been smeared by the wise man upon the blank page, unknown to anyone else.

When the disciple arrived at the abode of a venerable dervish, and told him of his experiences and desired to know the meaning of the blank pages, the dervish said:

'O one of great prospects! You were cured by the virtue in the page, not by the talisman.'

'But', said the disciple, 'why did I not know the secret of the blank pages?'

'When you are saving a life', said the dervish, 'it is the saving of the life which is important. The talk comes later.'

The disciple retraced his steps and sought the doctor who had treated him. The doctor had moved to a distant land, and it was only after many vicissitudes that he found him. He asked:

'What were the circumstances which led to your deciding to inscribe a talisman on paper for me, that day in the caravanserai?'

The doctor said:

'When I was the pupil of a great dervish who always concealed his miracles, he told me, ''One day you will be called to see a man lying sick in a caravanserai. If he has such-and-such a type of fever, call for plain paper and write a diagram on it. Then have him swallow the water in which the diagram has been immersed. His fever will abate in three hours.'' '

The disciple asked:

'Were you given any instructions about what to do if there was no paper?'

The physician said:

'My teacher said, when I asked him that, ''If there is no paper, it will be a man who has been heedless of his duty, one who is unmindful of the orders of sages. He will have brought death upon himself. If there is no paper there at that moment, the patient will die.'' '

Ansari's Answer

WHEN BAHAUDIN NAQSHBAND was sitting in his reception-hall one day, an insolent aristocrat, travelling in the service of a certain Sultan, demanded entry.

'Let him in,' said Bahaudin.

The envoy, after exchanging general salutations with the Maulana, said:

'One reason why I have made a detour to see you is to ask a very direct question. It is this: What exactly *is* your situation and status in life? I, for instance, can describe myself as an Amir, and I travel in the service of an Emperor.

'Other people are great lords, merchants, scholars and so on. Everyone has a designation in any civilized country. What are your pretensions, and what are we to call you? People call you a King (*Shah*) and a Lord, and also a Teacher. But the smallest literate with three boys in front of him is a teacher, and there are kings with no power at all beyond their name.'

Mirza Ansari said:

'Maulana, may I be permitted to answer this question?'

The Maulana said:

'If the Prince will accept your answer as sufficiently authoritative.'

The Prince said:

'Yes, for one does not usually ask anyone anything directly, if one can get information on the matter from an informed subordinate.'

Mirza Ansari said:

'Our Lord (Maulana) is a man who is visited by kings. Princes ask his advice. Aristocrats and scholars seek what he has to tell and show them. Merchants and nobles, commanders and even sultans sign themselves to him "Your Servant". So he has no rank which is below that of such people. He cannot be less than a sultan, whether he has the possession of land or not. He is not described as higher, because there is nobody higher to accord him this rank. My impression is that, by visiting him, you have not demeaned yourself. But you will have to ask someone greater than an emperor as to what his rank is, if we are to interpret it even in terms of this world.'

Maulana Bahaudin said:

'Would it not, therefore, be better to withdraw the question, since it seems to defy an answer?'

Two Pieces of Advice

ⲟⲩ

THERE WAS once a king who had been trying to treat his subjects with enlightened kindness and the minimum of control.

The people showed signs of disaffection and instead of showing co-operation and respect for the administration, became complaining and turbulent.

The king was standing on the ramparts of one of his castles one day in the midst of these preoccupations, when he saw a free dervish in a patched robe sitting on the ground below him.

The king thought:

'These dervishes are reputed to know all secrets: there will be no harm in seeking his counsel.'

He outlined his problem to the dervish, and said, 'I want a piece of advice in this matter.'

The dervish said:

'I shall give you not one piece, but two pieces of advice.'

'Thank you,' said the king, 'but all I need is one bit of advice.'

'In that case,' said the dervish, 'I would say to you: "If you must rule, then rule." '

So the king increased the power of his control over the people, and treated them with such severity that they revolted. Before very long he was forced to flee, and barely escaped with his life, disguised in a dervish robe.

He found himself in a forest where, stopping to wash his face in a stream, he saw the dervish who had advised him, sitting in contemplation. The king said, 'This is where your advice has brought me!'

'Would you like to hear the second piece of advice?' asked the dervish.

'I can lose nothing more, so I had better hear it,' said the king.

'The second piece of advice', said the dervish, 'is: "Never ask for advice, nor act upon it, without satisfying yourself that the giver of the advice is a qualified person." '

The Gifts

THREE PILGRIMS brought offerings to a Sufi teacher.

The first presented a flask of valuable perfume, the second a handkerchief in which were tied a number of gold coins, the third some rare spices, worth their weight in silver.

The Sufi put some of the perfume on the palms of his hands, he gave away the money to a passer-by, and he handed back the spices to the man who had brought them.

Some of the people who regularly went to observe the doings of the Sheikh discussed among themselves the meaning of these actions.

They decided that the gift of the perfume was accepted, and that this indicated favour for the giver, an acknowledgment of his spiritual attainments, real or to come; that the giving away of the gold meant that the sage was showing his indifference to material things; that the returning of the spices indicated a rebuff for the man who had offered them.

It was many years before the audience learned, since they were not initiated Sufis, of the real message behind the actions of the Sufi.

The explanation, given by a teaching-master, was this:

'The Sheikh had used the perfume to please the giver, since this man was still at the stage where he needed the support of worldly reward. He had given away the gold in order to teach the giver something which he lacked, which was real generosity. He had returned the spices to make the donor understand that possession of costly spices was nothing: it was the effort which had gone into their acquiring which mattered. And this effort it was which had already transformed that pilgrim and made him worthy to use the spices in still another way.'

How far is man in general from being able to interpret the

meaning of events! It is only in the circle of the elect that these things are understood.

*   *   *

It you are too superior a man to use a piece of string, do not be surprised if a rope is too large for the job.

Proverb

The Fox Who Was Made a Sufi

꘍ꕤ꘍ꕤ꘍ꕤ꘍ꕤ꘍ꕤ꘍ꕤ꘍ꕤ꘍ꕤ꘍ꕤ꘍ꕤ꘍ꕤ꘍ꕤ꘍ꕤ꘍ꕤ꘍ꕤ꘍ꕤ

A fox was raiding all the farms of a certain country, and carrying off chickens. The villagers called in a Sufi of great repute and asked him to help them by catching it.

He took out a charm and laid it in a certain place, and in quite a short time the fox was found helplessly rooted to the spot.

When the villagers saw this they were delighted. But as they gathered around, the Sufi took away the power of the charm and tied something on a collar around the fox's neck. Then, instead of handing it over to the people to be killed, he set it loose.

The villagers were in an uproar, and said, 'Whatever are you doing? Now the fox will start thieving all over again!'

'No,' said the Sufi, 'I have put the Symbol of the Way around his neck, and Sufis are not thieves, so he will not steal again, but confine his attentions to wild creatures.'

'But you could have killed him just as easily,' said the people.

'Ah,' said the Sufi, 'I needed him to have a little punishment, so that he might reform in thought as well as action.'

'But how can it be a punishment to give him the mark of the Sufi?'

'Don't you know? Well, now, whenever anyone sees him, they will drive him away from the haunts of men, saying, "You are irrational, an enemy of scholars. And scholars are—of course—the most wise of mankind." '

When a Man Comes To
See You . . .

BAHAUDIN NAQSHBAND said:

'When a man comes to see you, remember that his behaviour and his speech are a compound. He has not come to buy, to sell, to convince you, to give or to gain comfort, to understand or make you understand. He has almost invariably come to do or try to do all of these things and many more.

'Like the skins of an onion, he will peel off one depth after another. Finally, you will find, by what he says, what he is inwardly perceiving of you.

'When this time arrives, you will completely ignore the apparent substance and significance of his speech or actions, because you will be perceiving the reality beyond.

'Note well that the other individual, while he does this, is almost always totally unaware that he is talking the language of "the heart" (direct communication). He may imagine that there is a scholarly, cultural or other reason for his behaviour.

'This is the way in which the Sufi reads minds which cannot read themselves. In addition, the Sufi knows how competent at real understanding the other person is, how much he really knows— ignoring what he thinks he knows— and how much he really can progress.

'This is a major purpose of *sohbat* (human companionship).

Notes

These notes are of varying subject:
sometimes amplification of the theme,
sometimes book references, sometimes
biographical; some stories, too, have no
note at all, though not many, being
either self-explanatory or— in Sufi style
— entities in themselves which should
not be interfered with.

Although all Sufis are agreed that Sufism is a unity, scholars almost appear to vie with one another to find 'what it must have developed out of'. The following are some of the 'sources' and identifications claimed by a few specialists, who have succeeded only in showing that Sufism looks different to each one of them:

Gnostics: J. W. Redhouse, *The Mesnevi* (London, 1881), p. xiv.

Neo-platonism and Christianity: Gertrude Bell, *Poems from the Divan of Hafiz* (London, 1928), p. 49.

Shiah Islam, Shamanism, Christianity: Dr J. K. Birge, *The Bektashi Order of Dervishes* (Hartford, 1939), pp. 210 ff.

Brahmina and Buddhists, Beghards and Beguins: Rev. T. P. Hughes, *Dictionary of Islam* (Lahore, 1964 edition), p. 620.

Professor R. A. Nicholson is ultimately found to conclude: 'Sufism is undefinable' (*The Mystics of Islam* [London, 1914], p. 8).

These reactions dramatically illustrate the 'elephant in the dark syndrome' in which different men identify different parts of an elephant as a fan, a pillar, a rope, and so on. The original tale is given in my *Tales of the Dervishes* (London, Cape, 1967), p. 25 ff. and in *The Sufis* (London, Cape, 1969), from Hakim Sanai and Maulana Rumi.

SALUTE TO THE THIEF

Junaid of Baghdad (Abul-Qasim Junaid), ninth century. His Sufic name was Prince of the Group (*Sayed el-Taifa*). Impeccable in formal scholarship, he was for this styled Peacock of the Learned (*Taus el-Ulema*). He instructed his formal students in public and his mystical ones behind locked doors. He concentrated upon one of the eight formulations of Habib Ajami (eighth century) and this school was called Junaidist (*Junaidia*). Additional material in my *The Way of the Sufi* (London, Cape, 1968), p. 165 ff., 246.

THE CRITIC

The technique described here is not intended to replace ordinary human assessment procedure in problems, but to exercise an additional point of view than the obvious. Other examples of non-linear thinking are given in my *Reflections* (London, Octagon Press, 1968), *Caravan of Dreams* (London, Octagon Press, 1968), and *Wisdom of the Idiots* (London, Octagon Press, 1969).

THE MATERIALS OF THE LOCALITY

The reference is to 'Time, place, people' (*Zaman, Makan, Ikhwan*) — carrying on Sufi teaching in accordance with the real characteristics of a situation, not by reproducing dogmatic behaviour or other outward forms.

THE STRANGE BECOMES COMMONPLACE

Alim Azimi allows himself to be attacked, to dramatize a situation. This is known as the Malamati Technique: incurring reproach to illustrate its absurdity, or the shallowness of the attacker, or the superficiality of the assumptions of the audience. Further explanations in my *The Sufis* and *Tales of the Dervishes*.

INVISIBLE SERVICE

The argument that emotion can form a barrier to perception.

DISMISSED

Wrath employed for dynamic purposes, to move someone, not to humiliate him. Frequently used by Mulla Jami and Najmudin Kubra; see *The Sufis* and *Tales of the Dervishes*.

FOUR COMMUNITIES

Stressing the Sufi process of 'prescribing' according to the individual being dealt with, not applying training techniques regardless of the situation.

ACCUMULATED SUPPLICATIONS

Sufic contention that right intention concentrates inner power which can only benefit others with an equally right intention. But this doctrine denies the principle that 'if it feels good, it must be good'.

This completely cuts across all ordinarily comfortable beliefs that one can judge by appearances. A Malamati (capacity to incur blame for a higher purpose) procedure, this is strikingly unique among Sufis and is regarded by them as the reality of which masochism and revelling in 'holy suffering' is the degeneration or disease.

FULL CIRCLE

Not a didactic tale, this is a 'teaching story', intended to exercise the mind along unfamiliar pathways, rather than to cause a belief in a hidden mechanism. Those who take it in the second sense will be regarded by the Sufi as being too prone to imagination.

THE INSANE

Ajnabi ('The Stranger') frequently crops up in Sufic tradition as the one who tests sincerity. If money, respect or service, for instance, are given for outward show or personal satisfaction, this has to be revealed before the individual can make progress in finding his real self. Dervishes seeking to starve the 'artificial self' of lesser nutriment are generally working on these lines, and refuse gifts or honours.

A GROUP OF SUFIS

Such experiments as this are frequent in dervish lore; the aim being to reveal the superficialities of judging by social, not spiritual, criteria.

SALIK ON THE ROAD TO QANDAHAR

Illustrative action of this kind is traditionally employed to emphasize that hope and fear are manipulative factors, operating on a shallow level. Recent Western work on conditioning is only now slowly making these mechanisms known to the modern mind. Rabia el-Adawia coined the most repeated phrase on this subject when she said, 'Lord, if I worship you from fear of hell, plunge me into hell. If I worship you from hope of paradise, deny me paradise. I seek to worship you for yourself alone.' (See *The Way of the Sufi* and *The Sufis*.)

Halqavi transmits many 'demonstration-anecdotes' like this one. His important 'The Food of Paradise' (*Tales of the Dervishes*, pp. 15 ff.) was made into a children's book by Robert Graves and published in 1968 as *The Poor Boy who Followed his Star* (London, Cassell). As with many Sufi tales, the personalities (king, Sufi) in such interchanges are lay-figures standing for thought-processes. Rumi says in *The Mathnavi*, 'People say that these are stories which happened long ago. But naming "Moses" serves as an external appearance. Moses and Pharaoh are two of your entities, good man.'

THREE SUFI MASTERS

A recurrent Sufi theme that language has functions other than the overt meaning of the words. Sound may affect the brain (see my *Special Problems in the Study of Sufi Ideas* (London, Octagon Press, 1968), second edition, pp. 7–8); and in social situations an energy may be dissipated by another energy.

SECRET KNOWLEDGE

'Aversion therapy' is not a new discovery. This account describes a weeding-out process: first all who are easily influenced; then those who are obsessed. In this sense, Sufic selection of students differs completely from other methods which often seek the easily influenced whom they welcome as enlightened people, and also court the support of the obsessed. Further instances are contained in my *Caravan of Dreams* and *Wisdom of the Idiots*.

THE MOB

The Sufic capacity to detach from objects, thus preventing the development of 'idolatry' and fixations upon externals, has a survival, as well as a teaching, value. Baffled commentators trying to determine 'what Sufis believe', and encountering disavowals and contradictions, have been compelled by their own assumptions to regard Sufism as 'chaotic' or 'divided into different dogmas'. With the greater availability of Sufi materials in recent years in the West, and their study by observers without preconceptions, a fascinating pattern of assessment of Sufism is now emerging. Poets, as well as scientists, are discerning substance in the materials and not insisting upon being offered a narrow dogma to accept or reject. The distinguished poet Ted Hughes, for instance, says (in the *Listener*, London, October 29th, 1964), 'The Sufis, fifty million strong, must be the biggest society of sensible men there has ever been on earth.'

INVISIBLE

The Sufi action is invisible. Its literature, while vital, is not sacred. 'Sacred is that which cannot be destroyed' — Tayfuri.

AHMED YASAVI

Sufis work as much by exclusion as by inclusion of people, actions and ideas. Yasavi (died 1166) figures in both the Naqshbandi and Bektashi 'Chains of Transmission' of Sufism. He was a disciple of the Master Abu-Yusuf Hamadani (died 1140). A note on him is found in *Systematics* VI, March 4th, 1969, pp. 313–14. For his central teaching, see my *The Book of the Book* (London, Octagon Press, 1969).

THE STEAM OF THE POT OF IKHTIARI

Ikhtiari means 'The Man who has Choice'. Sheikh Imdad Hussein of the Qadiris has recently written on the confusion engendered in the East and the West by deliberate Sufi behaviour. (See *The Secret Garden of Mahmud Shabistari*, tr. by Johnson Pasha [London, Octagon Press, 1969].)

THE JOURNEY

This example of not prejudicing an action by concealing it from a participant is mirrored in several Sufi techniques described by fourteen orientalists in the Octagon Press symposium *New Research on Current Philosophical Systems* (London, 1968).

I DON'T KNOW

This tale from India makes a Hindu identify a Sufi better than his own followers can. A recent survey on Sufi theory and techniques connected with this feature is William Foster's *Sufi Studies Today* (London, Octagon Press, 1968 o.o.p.).

The unexpected in Sufi theory and action. See also R. W. Davidson's *Documents on Contemporary Dervish Communities* (London, Octagon Press, 1966).

THE WAY WHICH SEEMS TO LEAD TO WORTHLESSNESS...

Similar and connecting incidents are to be found in my *Reflections*, *Caravan of Dreams*, and *The Way of the Sufi*.

QUALITIES

Khidr, the 'invisible guide'. (See *The Sufis*, and *Caravan of Dreams*.) This very typical account from the Khidr corpus underlines the difference between imagined and real virtues.

ANWAR ABBASI

Stresses the choice between repute and effectiveness. The lay-figure Mulla Nasrudin (see my *The Exploits of the Incomparable Mulla Nasrudin* [London, Cape, 1966] and *The Pleasantries of the Incredible Mulla Nasrudin* [London, Cape, 1968]) is often used for this purpose.

PROTECTION

Sahl (son of Abdullah of Tustar) was a teacher of Mansur, the great martyr of the tenth century (see *The Sufis*). His followers were called Sahlis; dervishes in the phase of extreme effort (*mujahida*) are called Sahli, of Sahl.

THE ARISTOCRAT

The descendants of Mohammed include many of the Sufi teachers, including Abdul-Qadir of Gilan and Bahaudin Naqshband. The tradition of the family, however, demands that the supposed inherited capacities must be brought into reality by achievements in the ordinary world. (See William Foster's 'The Family of Hashim', in *Contemporary Review*, London, May 1960.)

GRIEF AND JOY

Self-observation involves analysis of grief and joy. This is not the same as introspection and worrying. Innumerable Sufi stories are designed for observation purposes.

THE MAGICIAN

This is one of the many Sufic anecdotes in this book which are believed to instruct on different levels—the factual one being the least important. Familiarization with prescribed Sufi literature may be an essential part of the student's preparation. The apparent paradox of the Sufi saying that 'the written word is meaningless' and also insisting upon its study is that the interpretation of the writings comes at a later stage than their study. As the Russian scholar M. Filshtinsky recently noted, the material is 'usually on two planes. The earthly in them is only the allegory of the heavenly ... In this mutual interchange of earthly and mystical planes lies the secret of the powerful influences exercised by the finest examples of Sufi lyrics.' (*Arabic Literature*, Academy of Sciences, Nauka, Moscow, 1966, p. 201.)

GRAMMAR

This tale, like some which follow it, being apparently critical of scholars, has traditionally produced energetic and indignant reactions from those who believe that academic activity and personality is being attacked. The purpose, however, is to reproach pedantry and shallow assumptions, at the worst, bad scholarship. The 'bad scholar' is the incarnation of the parallel poor operation of the mind. For other examples, see my *Wisdom of the Idiots*.

DISSATISFIED

Sufi thinking holds that essential, simple and higher truth underlies the complexities and verbiage found on 'lower levels'. The Sufic method of 'scatter', however, involves exposing the student to numerous extrapolations from this truth, so that an idea may build up in his mind: 'The known is the bridge to the unknown.'

CONVICTION

People who change their opinions generally imagine that they always do so for rational reasons. This has always been denied by Sufis, and recent research by Western investigators shows that there are other reasons for opinion change, previously unknown. Professor Ward Edwards (University of Michigan Engineering Psychology Laboratory) showed in 1969 that while people can reach a decision from facts given to them, they have great difficulty in altering these conclusions even when better evidence is presented to them.

THE LIGHT-TAKER

Sufi teaching primarily aims at preparing the student for experiences which would otherwise confuse and overwhelm him: 'The lower is transformed by contact with the higher.'

INTERPRETATION

The formal acceptance of a disciple by a master is not the beginning of the contact, but the external demonstration of a relationship which already exists. Sufis interact with pupils through exercises such as *Sohbat* (companionship) in which no word is spoken, when something is transferred from the master to the disciple. Such a concept would have seemed bizarre in the extreme to Western thinkers until recently. Dr E. R. John (in *Science*, vol. 159, p. 1489) reports how cats can 'learn' experiences from other cats by sheer association with them: 'It seems that our ancestors with their schemes of apprentices passively watching their masters, also "knew" — like the observer cats — what they were doing.' (Work at the Brain Research Laboratories at New York Medical College, reported in *New Scientist*, April 11th, 1968, p. 89.)

YUSUF SON OF HAYULA

Opposition to Sufism (known in Europe, and so styled by Roger Bacon in Britain, through Andalusia, as the Eastern Wisdom) has been continuous if unsuccessful in the East. Many current Western opinions of the Sufis are derived from this fact. See my *The Sufis*, *passim*.

IN CHINA

Sufi knowledge, as Rumi, Sanai and Ibn Arabi stress, bears little resemblance to the techniques and outward faces of 'religion', 'philosophy', 'mysticism' and other similar levels of study, though it is connected with them in a recognizable manner.

TO CAUSE ANNOYANCE

The Sufi is aware of the likely reaction of his correspondent, and builds this into his operation. This is an example of 'unperceived teaching'. It is more common to find examples of teaching where the Sufi master removes himself from the experiment entirely, to prevent subjective reactions. A recent report from Harvard Medical School (*The Times*, London, June 26th, 1969) entitled 'Psychiatrists make their patients ill', explains how the expectation of the individual causes him to act in a certain manner when he knows that the doctor is present or due to visit.

DISCOURAGING VISITORS

The necessity for a social or emotional ingredient in a teaching situation is denied by Sufis, in sharp contradiction of other persuasions, whose advocates invariably, in theory or reality, strive to include as many subjective and community ingredients as possible in 'teaching' contacts. An astonishing parallel to the Sufi insistence on the relatively greater power of subtle communication to affect man is found in scientific work which shows that all living things, including man, are 'incredibly sensitive' to waves of extraordinary weak energy—when more robust influences are excluded. (See M. Gauquelin's *The Cosmic Clocks* (London, P. Owen, 1969), p. 138 ff., 144 and 169, citing recent scientific work.)

BAHAUDIN

The forthrightness of Bahaudin Naqshband on occasion, as well as that of other Central Asian teachers, is typified in Jami (see *Tales of the Dervishes*) and Najmudin Kubra (see *The Sufis*).

READING

With a sufficiency of jealous pedants monopolizing, in traditional manner, public interest and often opposing Sufis in the manner recorded here, such an incident may well have happened in the past. But the tale is also intended to describe, in the persons of the 'scholars' and the 'horse', certain automatic mental processes.

EYES AND LIGHT

Salih of Merv was a noted Sufi of the nineteenth century. There is another traditional answer, often quoted of Sufis: 'The weakness of the owl's eyesight is not the fault of the sun.'

KASAB OF MAZAR

Kasab, meaning butcher, is a poetic name, signifying 'one who dismembers bodies of irrelevant assumption, to make their parts assimilable in the right manner'.

DIGESTION

The multiplicity of content and effect of Sufi teaching is characteristically emphasized here.

TARGET

Sufis receive no permission to teach until they are known to have no urge to teach which could be a mask for a desire for attention or power. 'Vocation', therefore, in Sufism, has a special meaning, and has no connection with the belief that one should spread the work. Teaching is, therefore, based upon capacity, not desire.

THE FOOD OF THE PEACOCK

This illustrates the Sufic theme that dervish lives contain work for the future as well as the present: 'Others sowed for me, I sow for others to come.'

THE PERFECT MAN

The effect, not the appearance, is the dervish aim. The psychiatrist A. Reza Arasteh's treatment of Jalaludin (*Rumi the Persian*, Lahore, 1965) stressing the importance of experience, not institution, is most interesting. Whether this study succeeds or not, its enthusiastic welcome by the redoubtable Dr Erich Fromm, and his recognition of Rumi as one with a 'profound insight into the nature of man', has contributed towards the present appreciation of Sufism as a higher study by man of man, and not—as formerly supposed —some kind of mystico-religious indoctrination system of a composite kind.

NOW BEGIN

This principle, that a phase of Sufi work is for specific communities and varies with the audience, is the one most often violated by 'institutionalized' Sufists: whose members, though more visible, are least recognizable by Sufis as Sufis.

A THOUSAND DINARS

This tale from Attar (see *The Sufis* for material on him) illustrates how a feeling of possession of money can accompany the believed detachment from it. Similar tales are to be found in *The Way of the Sufi*.

THE ORDEALS

Junaid, Shibli and Harari are three of the early classical masters. (See *The Sufis*, *Tales of the Dervishes* and *The Way of the Sufi*.)

MEN AND CAMELS

'As above, so below.' One of the numerous illustrations of Sufic perception in parable form.

ILLUSTRATIVE EXCLAMATIONS

As in many of the Nasrudin tales, the Sufi is miming the thought and behaviour of his audience, to give them an opportunity of examining it, as in a mirror. (See *The Exploits of the Incomparable Mulla Nasrudin*, and *The Pleasantries of the Incredible Mulla Nasrudin*.)

183

SUCCESS IN DISCIPLESHIP

'Capacity and not desire', most important factors in the Sufi quest. Aspiration may come first, but it must become effective through capacity if progress on the Path is to become possible.

POMEGRANATES

All real Sufi teachers test potential students to see whether they desire time, attention, comfort or even discomfort rather than knowledge and progress. This tale shows how time may be given for psychotherapy, not for illumination.

ABDALI

An illustration of the frequent condition, often unsuspected by the student, when he wants advantages, not instruction, from a teacher.

UNFETTERED

Nuri means 'of light', because he was said to shine in the dark while teaching. A disciple of Sari el-Saqati (see *The Sufis*), he died in A.D. 908. He was an associate of Junaid, who called him Spy of the Hearts (Jasus el-Qulub), because of his reputed capacity to read thoughts. One of his most remembered sayings is: 'This place—the earth—is for the service of God and for the attainment of unity with God.' His full name was Hadrat (the presence) Abul-Hussein Ahmad ibn Mohammed el-Nuri.

MUSA OF ISFAHAN

This Sufi capacity to be '*In* the world, not *of* it' is demonstrated in the astonishing number of adepts who are distinguished in mundane activities as well as important in Sufism. So marked is this release of worldly capacity that it has been regarded as illustrative of the difference between the Sufi and other type of mystic who opt out of the world or at most distinguish themselves in worldly affairs.   (See my *Oriental Magic*, London, Octagon Press, 1956, 1968.)

184

SANDALS

The carefully chosen courses for Sufi students which are found in teaching situations have often been taken by imitators to be systems for general application. Such remarks as this one by Ghulam-Shah should be read in this light.

STRUGGLE

'The Sufi finds his development-matter in analogy on any level of matter or substance' (Sheikh Nadaf).

THE YEMENITE INQUIRER

Sufi books are stated to be written not only for audiences limited in time; they also exercise functions not recognized in other cultures as those of books at all. One reason for so many Sufis acquiring personal copies of books is that many sheikhs have insisted that a book studied by more than one person has parted with some of its substance, and may have become depleted in some imperceptible manner.

MINAI'S JOURNEY

The existence of a concealed pattern in life is a frequent theme in Sufi tales. Minai means 'enameller'. (Cf. stories in *Tales of the Dervishes*, *Caravan of Dreams*, *Reflections* and *The Way of the Sufi*.)

ONLY THREE MEN IN THE WORLD

This striking tale of Khidr emphasizes two approaches to life: to dominate one's environment or to understand it before deciding where to harmonize and where to try to dominate.

THE PALACE OF THE MAN IN BLUE

Such expeditions as this—the dervish purposely testing people to see whether they display certain characteristics and whether they themselves perceive them—are frequent in the lives of the masters and in tasks set for disciples. (Cf. *Tales of the Dervishes, Caravan of Dreams*.)

THE MAN WHO WANTED KNOWLEDGE

It is widely believed, especially in the folklore tales which surround Sufism, that the real masters are 'cosmic agents of the Secret People', those who administer the earth for time immemorial and eternal purposes. (Cf. my *Destination Mecca* (London, Octagon Press, 1969) and *The Sufis*.)

THE MANTLE

A special form of memory-exercise is one of the Sufic 'practical philosophy' techniques.

UNWRITTEN HISTORY

The common error of confusing emotionality with religion or goodness, hallowed by its embedding in formalized and social-rooted thought, in fact lays man open to manipulation for different purposes, constructive or otherwise.

THE LEGEND OF THE CATTLEMAN

A parable of the rise, deterioration, secret refreshment and final degeneration of idea systems—whether in the individual or in an institution.

THE HANDICAP

This is an 'inner exercise' tale, designed to be absorbed and dwelt upon in meditation. The effect of such tales as this has been noted by several critics as being at one and the same time apparently banal, but yet capable of causing an acceptable effect upon the reader's mind. It is interesting to observe the unprompted reaction of thoughtful readers. The literary editor of the London *Evening News*, for example, says in regard to this type of material: 'You have to resist the initial impulse to dismiss this sort of thing as just pseudo-profundity and so give up at once. If you persevere, you discover that strange little bugs are laying eggs in your subconscious and after a day or two begin to hatch out—as modified behaviour.' ('A look at a Book', July 15th, 1969.)

HOW THINGS WORK

A meditation tale, for the purpose of making the mind familiar with certain structures of thought which relatively seldom occur in the ordinary way. Similar material is to be found in *Reflections* (second edition, London, 1969).

THREE VILLAGES

Not a didactic story, this tale is intended to enable the pupil's consciousness to dwell upon mental relationships made 'specific' as people and events. Sufis also shape such formats into tales to ensure their transmission through re-telling for entertainment purposes. Other examples are to be found in *Tales of the Dervishes, Wisdom of the Idiots* and *Caravan of Dreams*.

THE SUTRA OF NEGLECTFULNESS

A *sutra* is a screen or other object interposed between a person and a possible source of distraction during prayer. The word is used here to indicate that a sutra itself can become a cause of neglect as something which can attract attention at the expense of effective thinking.

REMEDY

This is a development meditation theme, and is not intended to have any commentary.

IN THE LAND OF FOOLS

This corpus of jokes is intended to exteriorize in human forms the patterns of individual thinking, and to explain that there are social incidents, real and possible, parallel to the mind's working. Geoffrey Grigson, the eminent literary critic, recently observed (*Country Life*, November 21st, 1968) a peculiar and advantageous psychological effect of Sufi 'jokes'; and went so far as to call them 'an addendum to language'.

MAN AND SUFI

Affirming the Sufi statement that man is largely a projection of his own fantasy, and does not yet behave like one. Mulla Nurudin Abdurrahman Jami (1414–92) was an illustrious Persian poet, Naqshbandi Sufi and Professor at a special college at Herat. He wrote *The Seven Thrones*, from which Lawrence of Arabia is said to have derived the name of his major work, *Seven Pillars of Wisdom*.

THE BOOK

A 'permeation tale' which Sufis of many orders are expected to know. Some aspects of special dervish tales are dealt with in my article 'The Teaching Story' (in the philosophical journal *Point*, winter 1968–9).

DERVISHOOD

This refers to a certain dervish mental 'succession-exercise' (here referred to as 'yesterday, today and tomorrow') designed to give the student the ability to lift his thinking into a cycle beyond the customary human rut.

THE REFLECTION CHAMBER AT DOSHAMBE

Underlines the uselessness of tasks if they become mere irksome duties, and the need to control extravagant attitudes towards a teacher. A Dar el Fikr chamber is regarded as an instrument, not as a place for aesthetic enjoyment.

LEARNING OF THE UNRIPE

An example of current history which is put into writing and kept for teaching purposes only with the master's permission. Such extracts are often given a date after which they may not be used, or the date from which they are 'active', which may have antedated the actual event. This custom causes chronologists endless perplexity in dating documents.

BRICKS AND WALLS

The ever-changing external form of Sufism, a source of the greatest confusion to well-meaning scholars, is concisely delineated here with this arresting parable.

THE HOLE AND THE THREAD

The total Sufi work often requires even great figures of the past to become, as time passes, only a part of a pattern of development. This doctrine of supercession permits the continued action of Sufis through alternative teachers, but deprives disciples of the satisfactions of personality worship. For the theory of 'the content, not the container', see my *The Book of the Book*, London, 1969.

THE SQUIRREL

The outward form of things, which includes their social aspect, though enjoyable to relatively ignorant participants, may be seen by a man of perception as causing affliction at another level, or blocking progress in another range. It is demonstration of this concept (not, as imagined, affection for insects) which caused some dervishes to attach bells to their shoes, 'to warn beetles of their approach'. So literal-minded are many chroniclers, imagining the figurative to mean the literal that such individuals would have assumed that Diogenes was indeed seeking a man with a light in the daytime, unless the interpretation had been carefully spelt out to them.

BAHAUDIN NAQSHBAND SAID:

Note by Bahaudin: 'Expectation is twofold: expectation of something anticipated, like sunrise, and expectation of something not yet experienced, like higher knowledge. Sufism deals with the latter. That is why Sufis prepare people for what they may expect.'

ONE OF OURS

'An argumentative man will not even enter paradise without a struggle.' — *Proverb*.

THREE REASONS

This tale has been taken to mean that the Sufis claim that they alone can survive the test of manipulation which they say is the means of maintaining formalized religion. But in Sufi schools the anecdote is employed to emphasize the claim that there is an additional function of mind which may be developed.

EXILE

An illustration of the absurdity of applying ordinary comparisons to the admitted relationship between 'this world and the other'. Authentic Sufi material on this theme is to be found in *Textos Sufis*, Kalendar, Buenos Aires, 1969.

THE MEDICINE

The teacher's instructions originate in an invisible pattern, and hence observance of any rules is of paramount importance. Some typical rules are given in my *Oriental Magic* (chapter 7) and in *The Sufis*. Imitators, observing dervish reluctance to introduce too many rules, have sometimes set up groups without any at all, with resultant chaos.

ANSARI'S ANSWER

The sovereignty of the Sufi community, and the precedence accorded in many places to its adepts is alluded to here. Traditionally the descendants of the Prophet (including Bahaudin) take social precedence over non-Hashemite monarchs, since no national authority can bestow or remove the Sharifian, or Sayed, title. (Cf. Sir Olaf Caroe, in *The Times*, London, November 25th, 1967, Letters to the Editor.)

THE GIFTS

This exercise is designed to instruct the student in how to avoid facile assumptions, and to observe situations more closely. Few people are as yet aware how traditional materials of this kind are receiving the attention of scientific researchers. An interesting recent example is the Research Memorandum *The Unfolding of Man* (EPRC–6747–3) by the distinguished Professor

Claudio Naranjo, carried out through the Stanford Research Institute and supported by the U.S. Office of Education, Bureau of Research, Washington. Only a few years ago, any investigation of 'human transformation' under such distinguished auspices would have been unthinkable.

THE FOX WHO WAS MADE A SUFI

A typical example of an entertaining anecdote including the exercise of thaumaturgical power often attributed to developed Sufis, with other interesting features. This tale is regarded in Sufi circles as also containing an important interior framework for mental development.

WHEN A MAN COMES TO SEE YOU ...

The Masters (*Khwajagan*) are noted for specializing in telepathic interchange with disciples and others. This method, apart from having other advantages, is believed to make it unnecessary to bypass subjective psychological conditions in suitable individuals, to enable 'heart to call to heart'.